KEYS TO INVESTING IN OPTIONS AND FUTURES

Second Edition

Nicholas G. Apostolou, DBA, CPA
Professor
Louisiana State University
Baton Rouge, Louisiana

BARRON'S

All inquiries should be addressed to:
Barron's Educational Series, Inc
250 Wireless Boulevard
Hauppauge, NY 11788

Library of Congress Catalog Card Number 95-18424

International Standard Book Number 0-8120-9005-5

Library of Congress Cataloging-in-Publication Data
Apostolou, Nicholas G.
    Keys to investing in options and futures / Nicholas G. Apostolou.
    — 2nd ed.
      p.   cm. — (Barron's business keys)
    Originally published: New York : Barron's Educational Series, 1991.
    Includes index.
    ISBN 0-8120-9005-5
    1. Options (Finance). 2. Futures. I. Title. II. Series.
HG6024.A3A66   1995
332.64'5—dc20   95-18424
                                        CIP

PRINTED IN THE UNITED STATES OF AMERICA

56789   9770   987

CONTENTS

INTRODUCTION

The financial markets have undergone tremendous change in the last twenty years. The markets have introduced a variety of financial instruments. None has been more exciting to investors than the expansion and growth of the options and futures markets. Both markets have captured the imagination of investors and dramatically altered the investment arena.

The growth of these markets has stunned even the most optimistic observers. Although the history of options extends back several centuries, it was not until 1973 that standardized, exchange-listed, and government-regulated options became available on the Chicago Board Options Exchange (CBOE). By the early 1980s, the daily volume of trading in stock options had reached the point where the number of shares underlying the options frequently exceeded the daily volume of shares traded on the New York Stock Exchange (NYSE).

A similar pattern exists in the futures market. The trading volume in futures has increased at a greater than 20 percent rate annually for the past twenty years. One estimate placed the dollar value of all futures contracts traded in the United States in 1994 at more than $15 trillion! The volume of Treasury bond futures alone is more than five times the volume of stocks traded on the New York Stock Exchange.

Options and futures are called derivative instruments. The term refers to the fact that the value of these instruments is derived from the stocks, bonds, indexes, currencies, etc., upon which they are based. Price moves in these instruments closely parallel what is occurring in the cash markets. In reality, traders in these instruments are also traders in the underlying securities.

Although most investors understand options and futures to be risky, speculative investments, they seldom appreciate their role as risk-management tools. These markets allow speculators to bear risk and hedgers to transfer risk. Hedgers are individuals and firms that make purchases and sales in these markets solely to establish a predetermined price level. Theoretically, the speculator assumes the price risk that the hedger is seeking to minimize. When the hedger sells futures, it is the speculator who buys; alternatively, when the hedger buys futures, it is the speculator who sells. A hedge is simply a transaction designed to minimize an existing or anticipated risk. Originally, the purpose of futures was to transfer risk from one party to another and to smooth out price fluctuations. Subsequently, speculation itself became an important factor in these markets. Speculators play an important role in making the options and futures markets more liquid by making it easier for those who buy and sell these instruments to execute trades.

Investors who wish to speculate in options and futures should be aware of the extreme risk involved. These investments are not for the casual investor. Most speculators in these markets lose money. Only sophisticated and disciplined speculators can expect to make consistent profit. It is possible to make quick profits with little capital and limit losses. However, a great deal of research and adherence to strict rules is required to make money consistently.

1

OPTIONS

A stock option is a contract that gives to its holder the right, but not the obligation, to buy or sell shares of the underlying security at a specified price on or before a given date. After this date, the option expires. Therefore, options contracts specify three conditions:

1. the property to be delivered
2. the price of the property
3. a specified period during which the right held by the buyer can be exercised.

Options have standardized terms, including the exercise price and the expiration time. This standardization makes it possible for buyers or writers (sellers) of options to close out their positions by offsetting sales and purchases. By selling an option with the same terms as the one purchased, or buying with the same terms as the one sold, an investor can liquidate a position at any time.

Options can be a versatile investment vehicle for investors who understand their risks and limitations. Strategies are not limited just to buying, selling, and staying out of the market. Options allow investors to tailor their positions to individual situations and be as conservative or as speculative as they wish. An investor can reap the following benefits from options:

1. protection of stock holdings from a decline in market price
2. increased income against current stock holdings
3. purchase of stock at a lower price
4. benefit to an investor from a big market move without knowing the direction of the move
5. benefit to an investor from the rise or fall of a stock without the cost of actually buying or selling the stock.

Since the creation of the Chicago Board Options Exchange (CBOE) in 1973, trading volume in stock options has grown remarkably. The listed option has become a practical investment vehicle for institutions and individuals seeking financial profit or protection. The CBOE is the world's largest options marketplace and the nation's second-largest securities exchange. Options are also traded on the American Stock Exchange (AMEX), the New York Stock Exchange (NYSE), the Pacific Stock Exchange (PSE), and the Philadelphia Stock Exchange (PHLX). Options are not limited to common stock. They are written on bonds, currencies, and various indexes. The CBOE trades options on listed and over-the-counter stocks, on Standard & Poor's 100 and 500 market indexes, on U.S. Treasury bonds and notes, on long-term and short-term interest rates, and on seven different foreign currencies.

Options traded on exchanges such as the CBOE are similar in many respects to common stock:

1. Options are listed securities.
2. Orders to buy and sell options are conducted through brokers in the same manner as orders to buy and sell stock. Similar to common stock, orders on listed options are auctioned on the trading floor of a national exchange.
3. Price, volume, and other information about options is almost instantly available.

The following are some crucial differences between common stock and options:

1. There is no fixed number of options. The number of available options depends upon the number of buyers and sellers.
2. There are no certificates as evidence of ownership. Printed statements prepared by the involved brokerage firms indicate ownership of options.
3. An option is a wasting asset. If it is not sold or exercised before expiration, it becomes worthless and the holder loses the full purchase price paid for the option.

2

OPTIONS TERMINOLOGY

The options market has a language all its own. Some of the more important terms include:

- *Options writer.* An options writer is the seller or issuer of an options contract. For example, if the buyer exercises an ABC call option, the options writer must deliver the required number of shares of ABC common stock. The options writer is sometimes called the options seller.
- *Options buyer or holder.* The options buyer is the investor who obtains the right specified in the options contract. For example, the buyer of an ABC call or put has the right, but not the obligation, to purchase or sell, respectively, shares of ABC Corporation common stock at a specified price within a specified period.
- *Exercise or striking (strike) price.* The exercise price is the price at which the holder can sell to or buy from the writer the item underlying the option. For example, an ABC 50 call option gives the buyer the right to purchase 100 shares of ABC stock at a price of $50 per share. On the other hand, an ABC 40 put option gives the buyer the right to sell 100 shares of ABC common stock at a price of $40 per share. In index options, settlement is made through the payment of cash rather than the delivery of property.
- *Expiration date.* The expiration date is the last date on which the buyer can exercise an option. If an option has not been exercised before expiration, it ceases to exist and is worthless. Options expire on the Saturday following the third Friday of the month in which they can be exercised.

3

- *Premium.* The premium is the price that the buyer of an option pays and the writer of the option receives. Premiums vary in response to such variables as the relationship between the exercise price and the current market value of the underlying security, the volatility of the underlying security, the amount of time remaining until expiration, current interest rates, and the effect of supply and demand in the options market. Options premiums are a nonrefundable payment from the options buyer to the options writer for the rights conveyed by the option.
- *Out-of-the-money option.* A call option is out of the money when the strike price is greater than the market price of the underlying interest. A put option is out of the money when the strike price is lower than the market price of the underlying interest. Premiums are lower when options are out of the money.
- *In-the-money option.* A call option is in the money when the strike price is less than the market price of the underlying interest. A put option is in the money when the strike price is greater than the market price of the underlying interest.
- *At-the-money option.* Options are at the money when the common stock price is equal to the strike price.
- *American-style and European-style options.* An American-style option can be exercised by the holder at any time after it is purchased until it expires. A European-style option may be exercised only on the expiration date. Almost all exchange-traded stock options are American-style. One exception are the interest-rate options traded on the CBOE.

3

CALL OPTIONS

A call option gives its holder the right to buy a specified number of shares of the underlying stock at a predetermined price (called the striking or exercise price) between the date of purchase and the option's expiration date. It must be emphasized that an option gives an investor the right to purchase, but not the obligation to do so. A single call option gives the holder the right to buy 100 shares. For example, an investor who bought an XYZ October 40 call option would have the right, but not the obligation, to buy 100 shares of XYZ common stock at a cost of $40 per share at any time before the option expires in October. The right to purchase common stock at a fixed price becomes more valuable as the price of the underlying common stock increases.

EXAMPLE:
Suppose you buy an XYZ 40 call option when the price of the stock is $40 and pay a premium of $2. A premium or price of $2 means that the option will cost $200 (an option contract is based upon 100 shares). If the price of XYZ stock climbs to $45 before expiration and the premium rises to $6, an investor has two choices in disposing of the option:

1. The option can be exercised and the underlying XYZ common stock can be bought for a total cost of $4,200 ($40 × 100 plus the $200 premium). The shares can then be sold for $4,500, yielding a net profit of $300.
2. The option contract can be sold for $600, earning a profit of $400 ($600 – $200 premium). Here, the investor makes a profit of 33⅓ percent (200/600), while the profit on an outright purchase given the

same price movement would be only 12½ percent ((45–40)/40).

An option does not have to be exercised to lock in profit. Like common stock, options are regularly bought and sold on the exchanges. Whether it is more advantageous to exercise or to sell a profitable option is influenced by whether an investor desires to own the common stock. In making the decision to exercise the option or to sell the stock, the investor must consider premium levels, commissions, and taxes. Unless the investor wants the stock, it is generally better to reap the profit by selling the option itself.

Of course, stock prices often don't move in the direction anticipated or desired. Using the previous example, assume that XYZ common stock fell to $35 and the option premium dropped to $75. You could sell the option to partially offset the $200 premium, and your loss would be $125. If you didn't take action, and the option expired worthless, your loss would be the total amount of the premium paid—$200. Yet, this loss would be less than if you had bought the 100 shares outright. An outright purchase would have produced a loss of $500 ($4,000 – $3,500).

Let's carry this example even further and assume that XYZ common stock has dropped to $30 per share and the option is worthless. Again, the loss to the option holder is $200, the total amount of the premium paid. However, if the shares had been purchased outright, the loss would have been $1,000 ($4,000 – $3,000).

These examples illustrate the two main advantages of options:

1. *Leverage.* A somewhat small investment controls a larger investment with corresponding greater profit potential.
2. *Limited and defined risk.* Despite how much XYZ stock falls, the maximum risk exposure is limited to the premium. In our example, the maximum loss that could be incurred on this option is the premium of $200.

4

PUT OPTIONS

A put option gives the holder the right to sell a specified number of shares of the underlying common stock at a predetermined price (striking or exercise price) on or before the expiration date of the contract. Buying an XYZ October 40 put gives an investor the right to sell 100 shares of XYZ stock at $40 per share at any time before the option expires in October.

EXAMPLE:

Assume that you buy an XYZ October 40 put at a premium of 2 (or $200) when the price of the underlying common shares is $40 per share. If the price of XYZ stock falls to $35 before October and the premium rises to 6, you have two choices in disposing of these in-the-money (the exercise price is greater than the market price) put options:

1. One hundred shares of XYZ stock can be purchased at $35 per share. Then, you can exercise your put option to sell XYZ at $40 per share. This produces a profit of $300 ($500 profit on the common stock minus the $200 option premium).
2. The put option contract can be sold, producing a profit of $400 ($600 premium received less the $200 premium paid).

As discussed previously, you don't have to exercise an option to realize the profit. It is generally a better strategy to sell an option than to exercise it. Sales of options usually involve lower transactions costs than exercising options.

If XYZ stock had climbed to $45 before expiration and the premium fell to 1, the option would be out of the money. You could continue to hold the option, hoping the price will drop, or sell it for $100. A sale for $100 would mean a $100 loss ($200 − $100). It is often a good strategy to sell an option at a loss rather than wait for the price of the stock to change in the investor's favor. The time value of an option rapidly shrinks toward zero starting about six weeks before expiration.

Short Sales vs. Put Options. An investor who anticipates declining stock prices can purchase put options or sell stock short. A *short sale* is the sale of a common stock that is not owned with the intention of repurchasing it later at a lower price. The investor borrows the stock from another investor through a broker and sells it in the market. Usually, a broker has other clients who own the security and are willing to loan shares.

An important aspect of a short sale order is that an investor does not receive the proceeds of the order at the time the trade is executed. In a short sale, the money is kept by the brokerage firm until the short is covered—that is, until the security is purchased and returned to the lender. Also, to ensure that the short position will be covered, the broker requires the posting of collateral. Most short selling is done through margin accounts, in which case short sellers are required to have in their accounts the required percentage of the stock's price (currently 50 percent).

The objectives of the put option purchaser are the same as those of the short seller. They are both trying to make a profit from declining stock prices. Unlike the short seller, however, the put buyer faces a maximum loss defined by the amount of the premium. A short seller lacks limits on the loss he/she can sustain. In addition, the short seller faces margin requirements and additional restrictions not applied to the put buyer. On the other hand, the option's limited life span constrains the put buyer. With options, an investor can be correct in anticipating future price changes, but still lose money because the price change did not occur within the limited period of the life of the option.

5

OPTIONS CLEARING CORPORATION

The Options Clearing Corporation (OCC) is the largest clearing organization in the world for options. A clearing organization guarantees that the terms of a contract—for example, an options contract—will be honored. In the options market, the OCC provides highly reliable clearance, settlement, and guarantee services. A wholly owned subsidiary, the Intermarket Clearing Corporation (ICC), provides the same benefits to the futures industry. The OCC is regulated by the Securities and Exchange Commission.

An options buyer looks to the OCC rather than to any particular options writer for performance. Similarly, the obligations of options writers are owed to the OCC rather than to any particular buyer. In other words, once the OCC is satisfied that there are matching orders from a buyer and a seller and that the premium has been paid, it severs the direct link between the parties and becomes the seller to the buyer and buyer to the seller. Since every options transaction involves both a buyer and a seller, the aggregate rights of options holders are matched by the aggregate obligations that options writers owe to the OCC.

This process benefits both the buyer and seller. The buyer and seller are free to act independently of each other. For example, the seller may buy the same option he/she has written, canceling out the initial transaction and terminating the obligation to deliver the stock. This action does not affect the right of the original buyer to sell, hold, or exercise that option. In addition, the OCC always guarantees all options that it issues.

The OCC was founded in 1973 as a clearing corporation for the Chicago Board Options Exchange (CBOE). The trading success of listed stock options at the CBOE encouraged other exchanges to enter the options marketplace. Currently, the OCC accepts and clears trades for six organizations: the CBOE, the American Stock Exchange (AMEX), the National Association of Securities Dealers (NASD), the New York Stock Exchange (NYSE), the Pacific Stock Exchange (PSE), and the Philadelphia Stock Exchange (PHLX).

In its role as the issuer and guarantor of listed options contracts, the OCC faces certain risks and performance obligations. To ensure the financial integrity of the markets it clears and to protect the interests of its members, the OCC has implemented a comprehensive series of safeguards, including rigorous membership standards, financial surveillance programs, margin requirements, and a clearing fund.

Each clearing member applicant is subject to an initial assessment of its operating capability and creditworthiness. Following receipt of an application and the necessary financial information, an on-site examination of the applicant's records and an operations orientation are conducted by the OCC staff. A recommendation is then submitted to the OCC's board of directors. Final approval for membership requires a majority vote by the board.

The OCC's financial surveillance programs are rigorous and continuous. Its surveillance staff members routinely:

1. monitor the operational and financial condition of each clearing member;
2. monitor general market conditions and the OCC's exposure with respect to specific clearing members on a daily basis;
3. evaluate the adequacy of the OCC's margin on a daily basis.

The OCC's first line of defense should a clearing member default is the margin deposit base for that member's account. Margin is the amount deposited as collateral for the writers' positions that a clearing member carries. The objective of the OCC's margin system is to accurately measure the OCC's exposure to risk and establish reserves that protect clearing members and the OCC against defaults. Rules established by the Margin Committee of the OCC state that an options seller must deposit either the underlying interest or maintain specified margin in the form of cash, U.S. government securities, bank letters of credit, or other acceptable securities.

The OCC's second line of defense is members' contributions to the clearing fund. The entire clearing fund is available to cover losses in the event that the margin and clearing fund deposits of the defaulting member are inadequate. The OCC's clearing fund totaled about $400 million at the end of 1994.

6

OPTIONS QUOTES

Major newspapers like *The Wall Street Journal* and *Investor's Business Daily* publish premiums (prices) for exchange-traded options. Exhibit 1 illustrates the information presented in the final market price quotations. Note that there are prices for different months. Exchange-listed options expire on the Saturday following the third Friday of the expiration month.

Originally, all exchange-traded options expired according to one of three standard expiration cycles:

1. January/April/July/October
2. February/May/August/November
3. March/June/September/December

This simple expiration cycle, however, was changed by the exchanges because they found that the most actively traded contracts were the ones with the shortest terms. All equity options still have four expiration months. These months are the nearest two plus two additional taken from one of the original standard expiration cycles. Therefore, stocks have options with four different expiration months, even though many newspapers only show the quotes for the closest three months. To illustrate, a stock from the January cycle would have the following trading months available after the January expiration: February, March, April, and July. Since each stock has four expiration months trading simultaneously, an individual stock may have as many as four puts and four calls with the same exercise price, but different expiration dates. For example, Merck could trade February 70s, March 70s, April 70s, and July 70s.

Note also the trading in options with a common expiration date but different exercise prices. For example, in the exhibit, Merck has 60s, 65s, 70s, 75s, and 80s all expiring in October. The different exercise (striking) prices are introduced when there is a significant change in the underlying stock price. New exercise prices for stock options are usually introduced at 2½-point intervals for stocks trading below 25, at 5-point intervals for stocks trading from 25 to 200, and at 10-point intervals for stocks trading above 200. New listings are added when a stock reaches the high or low striking price.

EXAMPLE:
Stock options with exercise prices of $30, $35, and $40 are introduced when the stock is trading at $35 per share. If the stock should drop to $30, new options are introduced with a $25 exercise price. If the stock price should thereafter rise to $40, additional options with an exercise price of $45 would be introduced. A long list of striking prices indicates that the stock has moved over a wide range.

Premiums are quoted in multiples of $\frac{1}{16}$ for options priced below $3, and $\frac{1}{8}$ for other options. To a large extent, the premium is the central focus of options trading. Most investors wish to purchase an option when the premium is low and sell the same option at a higher premium. Alternatively, for options writers, the premium received is a source of additional income or a hedge against a possible decline in the price of stocks owned or to be purchased.

Exhibit 1
How to Read Options Quotations

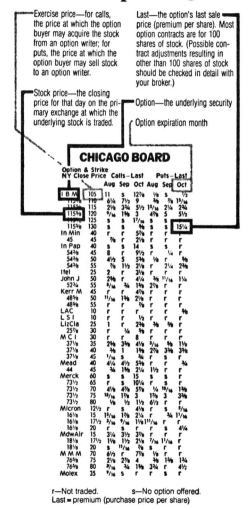

Exercise price—for calls, the price at which the option buyer may acquire the stock from an option writer; for puts, the price at which the option buyer may sell stock to an option writer.

Last—the option's last sale price (premium per share). Most option contracts are for 100 shares of stock. (Possible contract adjustments resulting in other than 100 shares of stock should be checked in detail with your broker.)

Stock price—the closing price for that day on the primary exchange at which the underlying stock is traded.

Option—the underlying security

Option expiration month

CHICAGO BOARD

Option & NY Close	Strike Price	Calls—Last Aug	Sep	Oct	Puts—Last Aug	Sep	Oct
I B M	105	11	s	12 7/8	1/8	s	1/2
115 5/8	110	6 1/4	7 1/2	9	3/8	7/8	1 5/16
115 5/8	115	2 1/8	3 3/4	5 1/2	1 5/16	2 1/4	2 3/4
115 5/8	120	9/16	1 5/8	3	4 7/8	5	5 1/2
115 5/8	125	s	s	1 7/16	s	s	[illegible]
115 5/8	130	s	s	5/8	s	s	15 1/4
In Min	40	r	r	5 7/8	r	r	[illegible]
45	45	7/8	r	2 1/8	r	r	r
In Pap	40	s	s	14	s	s	r
54 3/8	45	8	r	9 1/2	r	1/4	r
54 3/8	50	4 1/2	5	5 3/8	1/8	r	5/8
54 3/8	55	7/8	1 1/2	2 1/8	r	2 1/4	2 3/8
Itel	25	2	r	3 1/8	r	r	r
John J	50	2 5/8	r	4 1/4	3/8	11/16	1 1/4
52 3/4	55	5/16	3/4	1 5/8	2 7/8	r	r
Kerr M	45	r	r	4 7/8	r	r	r
48 5/8	50	11/16	1 3/8	2 1/8	r	r	r
48 5/8	55	r	r	7/8	r	r	r
LAC	10	r	r	r	r	r	5/8
L S I	10	r	r	1/2	r	r	r
LizCla	25	1	r	2 3/8	3/8	5/8	r
25 7/8	30	r	1/4	5/8	r	r	r
M C I	30	r	r	8	r	r	r
37 1/8	35	2 5/8	3 3/8	4 1/8	3/16	5/8	1 1/8
37 1/8	40	3/8	1	1 5/8	2 7/8	3 3/8	3 5/8
37 1/8	45	1/16	s	3/4	r	s	r
Mead	40	4 1/4	4 1/2	5 3/8	r	r	3/4
44	45	3/4	1 5/8	2 1/4	1 1/2	r	r
Merck	60	s	s	15	s	s	r
73 1/2	65	r	s	10 1/4	r	s	r
73 1/2	70	4 1/8	4 7/8	5 7/8	1/4	13/16	1 3/8
73 1/2	75	13/16	1 7/8	3	1 7/8	3	3 3/8
73 1/2	80	1/8	1/2	1 1/2	6 1/2	r	r
Micron	12 1/2	r	s	4 1/8	r	s	5/16
16 1/8	15	1 5/16	1 7/8	2 1/4	r	3/4	1 1/16
16 1/8	17 1/2	3/16	9/16	1 1/8	1 11/16	r	r
16 1/8	20	r	s	r	r	s	4 1/4
MdwAir	15	3 1/4	3 1/2	3 7/8	r	r	r
18 1/8	17 1/2	1 1/8	1 1/2	2 1/8	7/16	1 1/16	r
18 1/8	20	s	11/16	7/8	s	r	r
M M M	70	6 1/2	r	7 7/8	1/8	r	r
76 5/8	75	2 1/8	2 7/8	4	3/8	1 3/8	1 3/4
76 5/8	80	3/16	3/4	1 5/8	3 3/4	r	4 1/2
Molex	35	9/16	s	r	r	s	r

r—Not traded. s—No option offered.
Last = premium (purchase price per share)

Source: *Understanding Options*, Chicago Board Options Exchange, Chicago, IL, 1989, p. 12.

7

VALUATION OF
CALL OPTIONS

Six factors determine the value of an American call option. Recall that an American call option may be exercised at any time before the expiration date, whereas a European option may be exercised only on the expiration date. Premiums are determined by the relationship to:

Stock price. The call's price rises when the price of the stock rises, and falls when the price of the stock falls. The relationship is based upon the fact that an option represents a levered position in the underlying stock. A relatively small initial premium gains control of a larger asset with significant profit potential.

A call option has intrinsic value if the stock price is greater than the exercise or striking price At a given exercise price, the price of the common stock determines whether the option is in the money (stock price > exercise price) and therefore has intrinsic value, or out of the money (stock price < exercise price) and has only time value (the option's premium above any intrinsic value).

Cash dividends. The value of a call option is inversely related to the dividends paid on the common stock. To illustrate, consider what happens on the ex-dividend date. On this date, stockholders are not eligible to receive the dividend and the market price on the opening sale is reduced by the amount of the dividend. Since the stock's price declines by the amount of the dividend, the call option price should drop in a corresponding fashion.

Stock price volatility. A positive relationship exists between the volatility of the underlying stock and the value of the call option. The greater the volatility, the greater the potential that the call option will gain intrinsic value and be in the money. In other words, volatile stocks have greater movement, which increases the likelihood that at some time before the option expires, it will be in the money. If the call option is in the money at expiration, it will be profitable for the holder to exercise the option.

Time to maturity. A major determinant of the value of an option is its time to maturity. The longer the period to maturity, the greater the value of the option. The longer the time frame, the greater the chance that options will gain intrinsic value. This relationship is why longer-term call options on a given common stock and exercise price will have higher prices than shorter-term options.

Exercise price. The call option price is higher when the exercise price is lower, and lower when the exercise price is higher. Call options of the same price and with identical maturities will have different values because of their different exercise prices. Out-of-the-money call options have lower premiums because they have lower intrinsic values. As call options go in the money, their intrinsic values increase and the premiums rise. For example, consider a common stock trading at $60 per share. A call option with an exercise price of $50 has a greater value than a call option with an exercise price of $55. The $50 option is in the money by $10 while the $55 option is in the money by only $5.

Interest rates. The final factor is the positive relationship between the market interest rate and the value of a call option. Higher interest rates produce higher call option prices, while lower interest rates result in lower call option prices. In effect, a call option buyer's levered position is being financed by a loan from a call option writer. The call option writer defers the benefits of converting the stock to cash by enabling the options buyer to lever his/her position in the common stock. Higher interest rates mean that the opportunity cost of entering the agreement with the options buyer is greater for the options seller. Therefore, an options writer will demand a higher call option premium to compensate for the inability to take advantage of the higher interest rates.

Intrinsic Value and Time Value. The value of an option consists of two components: intrinsic value and time value. *Intrinsic value* reflects the amount by which an option is in the money. For example, when the market price of ABC stock is $56 per share, an ABC 50 call option has an intrinsic value of $6. If the underlying stock declines to $52, the intrinsic value of the call option is only $2. However, if the price of the underlying stock drops to $50 or less, the call option lacks intrinsic value.

Time value is the value an option has in addition to its intrinsic value. It reflects what the buyer is willing to pay for an option in anticipation of price increases before expiration. For example, when the market price of ABC common stock is $50 per share, an ABC 50 call option may command a premium of $2. This premium is entirely time value; it reflects the hope that the underlying security will rise sufficiently to enable the holder to sell or exercise the option. The time value of an option typically decreases as the option approaches expiration and eventually becomes worthless. Just before the option's expiration date, its premium is either zero or its intrinsic value. At this point, its time value is zero, and the option price or premium is solely determined by its intrinsic value. The components of the premium may be expressed by this formula:

Option Premium = Intrinsic Value + Time Value

This formula applies to both put and call options. For in-the-money options, the time value is the amount over intrinsic value. For at-the-money and out-of-the-money options, the time value is the option premium.

8

VALUATION OF
PUT OPTIONS

Like all items traded in a competitive economy, the supply and demand for an option determines the price or premium of the option. During periods of rising stock prices, the demand for calls grows stronger and call premiums tend to rise. During periods of declining or stable prices, call premiums tend to be lower. Alternatively, strong stock prices tend to reduce the demand for puts, and put premiums tend to decline, while weak stock prices generally increase the demand for puts, exerting upward pressure on put premiums.

Although this analysis provides a general explanation for changes in premiums, more specific factors can be defined that primarily account for the changes in put option prices. These factors are the same factors that affect call option prices. They include:

Stock price. The value of a put option rises when the price of the stock falls, and falls when the price of the stock rises. At a given exercise price, the price of the stock determines whether the option is in the money and has intrinsic value or if it is out of the money and has only time value. Since a put option grants the right to sell shares at the exercise price, this right becomes less valuable to the owner as the stock price rises and the put option loses intrinsic value. If the price of the underlying common stock declines, the put option gains intrinsic value.

Exercise price. The value of a put option is greater the higher the exercise price, and smaller the lower the exercise price. This relationship exists because put options gain intrinsic value as exercise prices increase. In other words, for a given stock price, the higher the exercise price is, the greater the value of a put. For example, assume a stock sells for $50. A put option with an exercise price of $60 has a higher value than an option with an exercise price of $55. The first is in the money by $10, while the second is in the money by only $5.

Cash dividends. The put option's value increases when the underlying common stock pays cash dividends. A stock's price should decline by the amount of the cash dividend on the ex-dividend date. The ex-dividend date is the period during which purchasers of the stock cannot receive the next quarterly dividend.

Time to maturity. A significant factor in determining the premium of a put option is the time to maturity. The longer the time to maturity, the greater the value of the option. Longer-term put options command higher premiums. The put option's time value slowly declines until about six weeks before expiration. After that, the dissipation of time value accelerates.

Interest rates. Put option prices rise when interest rates fall, and fall when interest rates rise. One way to explain this relationship is to use the present value argument. The premium on the put option reflects the present value of the exercise price. The higher the interest rate, the lower the present value of the exercise price and the lower the intrinsic value of the option. Lower intrinsic values translate into lower premiums. Alternatively, lower interest rates increase the present value of the exercise price, which increases intrinsic value. A higher intrinsic value results in higher premiums.

Stock price volatility. The last factor is the volatility of the underlying stock price. The more volatile the stock, the higher the price of the put option. The greater the volatility of the stock price, the greater the potential for the option to gain intrinsic value. Volatility is nondirectional in that the fluctuation could be up or down. Consequently, when higher volatility is expected, premiums on both puts and calls rise.

9

DELTAS

A key concept in options theory is delta. Delta measures the change in an option's price (premium) relative to the change in the underlying price of the stock. Call option deltas are positive and put option deltas are negative, since call options have a positive relationship and put options a negative relationship with the underlying stock's price. Call option deltas usually range in value from 0 to 1, while put option deltas generally range from 0 to –1. A call delta of 0.50 indicates that a one-point increase in the stock should be accompanied by a ½-point increase in the call premium. For a put with a delta of –0.25, a one-point increase in the stock produces a ¼-point drop in the put premium. A higher delta indicates that a call option price will have a greater reaction to a rise or fall in the price of a stock. Conversely, the lower the delta, the more responsive put premiums are to changes in the price of a stock.

At-the-money (price of the stock = exercise price) call and put options have deltas of approximately +½ and –½, respectively. Deep-in-the-money call options (underlying stock is more than 5 points above the exercise price) have deltas that approximate +1 and deep-in-the-money put options (underlying stock is more than 5 points below the striking price) have deltas of approximately –1. When option positions are deep out of the money, their deltas approach zero.

EXAMPLE:
The striking price of a call is $40, and the underlying stock is currently priced at $49. This call is deep in the money and its delta should approach 1. The premium should experience a $1 price increase for each $1 gain in

the price of the stock. Premiums for deep-in-the-money options consist almost entirely of intrinsic value and are almost perfect surrogates for positions in the underlying stock.

EXAMPLE:

The striking price of a call is $40, and the underlying stock is currently valued at $40. This call is at the money and its delta should approximate $+\frac{1}{2}$. A 1-point change in the price of the stock should produce a $\frac{1}{2}$-point change in the premium. This option has no intrinsic value currently, but has the potential to gain intrinsic value in the future. The delta value of $+\frac{1}{2}$ reflects this profit potential.

EXAMPLE:

A call has an exercise price of $55, and the stock is currently priced at $43. This deep-out-of-the-money options delta approaches 0. A +1-point movement in the stock will have little or no effect on the premium. Deep-out-of-the-money options have no intrinsic value, extremely small deltas, and little chance of being exercised by the holder.

Investors should assess their risks in options daily. Computing deltas forces investors to confront the risk they are assuming in trading options. Observing an option's premium in relationship to changes in the price of stock can often spotlight distortions in time value (amount by which the premium exceeds intrinsic value).

EXAMPLE:

An investor ⌄wns 100 shares of common stock purchased at $50 per share. Three weeks later, the stock has risen from $50 to $53, following a takeover rumor. The 50 call option rose from 3 to 7, an increase of 4 points. The delta would show a value of 1.33 ($\frac{4}{3}$).

An option's delta can be used in managing risk. The delta tells the investor who owns options the number of shares required to construct a position that will protect the investor from the effects of price movements in the underlying stock. The combination of options and stock to create such a position is called a *delta-neutral.* The total value of the position will remain stable despite changes in the prices of the individual components.

For example, suppose that XYZ's common stock is trading at 41, and the 3-month put options and call options, with exercise prices of 40, have prices of 2 and 4, respectively. Assume that the call option's delta is 0.70. Since the put option is the obverse of the call option, its delta can be computed by subtracting 1 from the call's delta. Therefore, the put option's delta in this case is –0.30 (0.70 – 1.00). These numbers imply that a \$1 increase in the price of the stock will increase the call option's price by \$0.70 and reduce the put option's price by \$0.30. A delta-neutral call position can be created by purchasing 70 shares of XYZ stock for every call option sold, whereas a delta-neutral put option can be produced by purchasing 30 shares of stock for every put option purchased.

10

COVERED CALL WRITING

Investors have been using two strategies involving stock options to offset risk. These strategies are covered call writing and protective puts. The strategy of choice for an investor is dependent upon the extent of the expected stock or stock market decline.

Many investors view options as highly speculative, risky investments. However, there are several options strategies that are conservative. One such strategy is covered call writing. Investors write covered calls for the following two reasons:

1. to realize additional income on the underlying common stock by earning premium income;
2. to provide a measure of downside protection (limited to the amount of the premium) against small declines in the price of the stock.

Covered call writing is usually considered to be a more conservative strategy than the outright purchase of common stock, because the investor's downside risk is reduced by the amount of the premium he/she receives for selling the call.

The covered call writer either buys common stock and simultaneously sells an equivalent number of call options against the shares purchased (commonly called a "buy-write"), or sells calls against common stock that is already owned. Any investor can profit from this strategy. Its characteristics can be summarized as follows:

1. The sale of the option provides immediate cash flow.
2. Losses are reduced by the amount of the premium in the event of a downward movement in the price of the common stock.

3. It provides a good return even if the underlying common stock is called away (exercised).

A covered call writer owns the underlying common stock but is willing to give up price increases in excess of the option stock price in return for the premium. An investor should be prepared to deliver the common stock shares, if assigned, at any time during the life of the option. (Assignment is the receipt of an exercise notice by an options writer that obligates him or her to sell the underlying security at the specified exercise price.) To avoid losing the stock, an investor may cancel his or her obligation at any time by executing a closing transaction. A closing transaction is performed by buying a call in the same series (options with identical terms).

EXAMPLE:
Let's look at an example of covered call writing provided by the New York Stock Exchange in a booklet titled *NYSE Options:*

1. Buy 200 shares XYZ at $28	$5,600
2. Less option premium for 2 April 30 calls	– 600
3. Net investment	$5,000

The gain or loss from possible price movements can be illustrated as follows ($28 = stock purchase price):

- 30 ↑ Gains cease above 30 (I)
- 30   Maximum gain realized if stock rises to stock price (II)
- 28   Return increased by the amount of the premium as option expires (III)
- 25   Premium received acts as a downward cushion to breakeven point (IV)
- 25 ↓ Dollar-for-dollar loss beyond breakeven point (V)

In three of the five possible scenarios, covered writing provides greater profits than outright stock ownership:

I. If the common stock climbs above 30, the investor will not participate in the advance above 30 as the stock will be exercised.

II. Maximum profit potential (if stock reaches $30)

a. Sell 200 shares at striking price 30	+6,000
b. Less initial purchase	−5,600
c. Gain in stock	400
d. Plus premium received	600
e. Net profit	+ 1,000

III. Stock price is unchanged

a. Stock remains at 28	5,600
b. Less initial purchase	−5,600
c. Gain on stock	0
d. Plus option premium received	600
e. Net profit on initial purchase	+ 600

IV. A price decline to breakeven point

a. Net investment	5,000
b. Divide total by number of shares purchased (5000/200)	25

V. If the stock drops below the breakeven point, the investor will suffer a dollar-for-dollar loss below 25.

11

UNCOVERED CALL WRITING

Uncovered—or naked—call writing differs from covered call writing in that the investor does not own the shares of the common stock represented by the option. The objective of the writer of an uncovered call is to earn a return from the writing transaction without committing money to the ownership of the underlying shares of stock. An uncovered call writer must deposit and maintain enough margin with his/her broker to guarantee that the stock can be purchased for delivery if the call is exercised.

Writing uncovered calls can be profitable during periods of declining or generally stable prices, but investors who are considering this strategy should be aware of the significant risks involved. If the market price of the underlying common stock sharply increases, the call could be exercised. To satisfy the delivery obligation, the writer would have to acquire stock in the market for substantially more than the exercise price of the option. This action could result in a large net loss. Therefore, uncovered call writing should be undertaken only by investors who have studied the options market closely and are financially able to afford the risk.

To illustrate, an investor who writes an XYZ October 40 call for a premium of 4 receives $400 in premium income. If the stock price remains at or below $40, the calls will not be exercised. However, if the stock price rises to $55, the investor will be assigned and will incur a loss of $1,100 ($1,500 loss on covering the call assignment less the $400 premium). An uncovered call writer may cancel the obligation at any time prior to being assigned by executing a closing purchase transaction (buying a call ir the same series).

12

PROTECTIVE PUTS

A protective put is the simultaneous purchase of a stock and a put option or the purchase of a put related to a stock already owned by the investor. Whereas covered call writing provides a partial hedge against a decline in stock prices, protective puts can provide almost complete protection. If the stock should decline, the price of the put should increase, especially when the put is in the money.

A protective put results in unlimited profit potential. The price of protection against loss while retaining the upside potential is the put option's premium. Since the put option is a right to sell at a predetermined price, the purchase of the put predetermines the maximum risk of the stock. This limit of the risk occurs because a put entitles the investor to sell the underlying shares at the exercise price of the put at any time through the expiration of the option, despite how much the price of the common stock declines. Yet the investor continues to receive any dividends paid during the period on stock owned. For common stocks that pay substantial dividends, this dividend revenue can substantially reduce the cost of purchasing puts.

The cost of protection can be measured in terms of annualized percent of investment. For example, consider a six-month XYZ put with a premium of 4 when the stock is trading at $50. The premium of 4 represents 8 percent of the $50 cost of XYZ. Since the 8 percent premium protects the investor for only six months, the annualized cost of protection is 16 percent. The 16 percent annual cost is the price the investor is willing to pay to benefit from any advance in the stock of XYZ, while limiting the risk.

The protective put strategy is most effective when the investor feels the price of the stock is vulnerable on the

27

downside. In employing this strategy, the investor probably should stick to the put whose exercise price is closest to the existing price of the common stock. In addition, it is advisable to purchase a put with at least three months remaining to expiration. This strategy permits the stock sufficient time to make an upward move.

Let's examine this strategy by considering the following example:

EXAMPLE:

1. Buy 200 shares XYZ at 40	$8,000
2. Buy 2 six-month XYZ 40 puts at 3	600
3. Net investment	$8,600

The cost of the transaction is $43 ($8,600/200 shares) per share. The purchased puts give the investor the right to sell the shares at $40 at any time up to expiration, no matter what happens to the price of the stock. The premium defines the maximum risk of loss, which in this case is the $3 ($600 in total) price of the put.

The possible price movements and the effect on profits can be illustrated as follows: ($40 = stock purchase price)

- 43 ↑ Potentially unlimited gain over $43 (I)
- 43   Breakeven point (II)
- 40   Premium of $600 is lost as option expires worthless (III)
- 40 ↓ Maximum loss is the cost of the put premium (IV)

28

I. Maximum gain realized if stock rises above $43. Assume the price of the stock hits $50, resulting in the put's becoming worthless.

a. Sell 200 XYZ at $50	$10,000
b. Less initial purchase	8,600
c. Net profit on initial investment	$ 1,400

II. Breakeven position

a. Sell 200 XYZ at 43	$ 8,600
b. Less initial purchase	8,600
c. Net profit	$ 0

III. Stock price remains unchanged

a. Sell 200 XYZ at $40	$ 8,000
b. Less initial purchase	8,600
c. Net loss on initial purchase (the price of the put)	– $ 600

IV. Stock declines in price, for example, to $30. The puts can be exercised to sell 200 shares of XYZ at $40 per share. The use of puts limits the loss to the premium paid of $600 rather than the $2,000 loss had the puts not been purchased.

a. Exercise puts by selling 200 XYZ at $40	$ 8,000
b. Less initial purchase cost	8,600
c. Net loss	–$ 600

13

WRITING PUT OPTIONS

The seller (or writer) of a put option is obligated to purchase the underlying stock—normally 100 shares—at the exercise price upon receipt of an exercise notice. In return for assuming this risk, the investor is paid a premium at the time the put is written. As a put writer, the investor must be prepared to buy the underlying stock at any time during the life of the option.

A put writer is considered to be *covered* if he/she has a corresponding short position or has cash deposits or cash equivalents equal to the exercise value of the option with his/her broker. Recall that a short sale is the sale of a security that is not owned with the intention of repurchasing it later at a lower price. The investor borrows the stock from another investor through a broker and sells it in the market. Subsequently, the investor repurchases the stock and returns it to the broker. To ensure that the short position is covered, the broker requires the posting of collateral.

A covered put writer's profit potential is limited to the premium received and the difference between the exercise price of the put and original price of the stock shorted. The potential loss on this position is substantial: the price of the stock may increase significantly above the original price of the stock shorted. In this case, the short position will generate losses offset only by the premium received. The covered put writing strategy is not used frequently, because uncovered put writing offers the same risk and rewards with generally higher premiums.

A put writer is considered to be *uncovered* if he/she does not have a corresponding short stock position or has not deposited cash or cash equivalents equal to the exercise value of the put. An investor unwilling to purchase stock at the current price might write put options, hoping to acquire the stock at a lower price and, meanwhile, receive premium income. If the put is exercised, the cost of the common stock will be the exercise price less the premium.

EXAMPLE:

The current market price of XYZ is $40 per share. An investor who owns 500 shares would like to acquire 200 more shares at $35 per share. The investor writes two puts with an exercise price of $40 at a premium of $5 per share. Assume that the price of the stock drops to $38 per share and the put is exercised. The investor's cost of acquiring the 200 shares of common stock is $35 per share (the $40 exercise price less the $5 put premium).

In this example, the cost to acquire the shares ($35) is under the current market value of the stock. If the stock declines further, the acquisition price could exceed the market value. This risk explains why this strategy should be used only by sophisticated investors with substantial financial resources.

EXAMPLE:

Suppose the stock in the previous example drops to $20 and the put is exercised. The put writer's $35 cost of acquiring the stock substantially exceeds the current market value of $20.

If the stock in the example increased in price, the put would not be exercised. The investor would have a profit determined by the premium. However, if the stock had advanced $3 to $43 by expiration, the investor could purchase the stock at a net cost of $38 ($43 – $5 premium), which is less than the market price of the stock when the option was written.

14

STOCK INDEXES

Stock market indexes were developed to measure performance of the stock market. Most investors gauge the state of the stock market from the news media reports of the Dow Jones averages and the Standard & Poor's (S&P) 500 Index. Index options were introduced in March 1983, when the Chicago Board Options Exchange (CBOE) began trading options on the Standard & Poor's 100 Index (S&P 100). Shortly thereafter, the American Stock Exchange followed with an options contract on the Major Market Index, and the New York Stock Exchange introduced options on the New York Stock Exchange Composite Index. Within one year of trading, index options accounted for over half of the volume of all options traded, and daily volume in the options exceeded $4 billion in the underlying commons stock.

S&P 100 Index. The most popular stock index option and the most actively traded of all options is the S&P 100 Index option, which is traded on the CBOE. The S&P 100 Index is composed of one hundred blue-chip stocks on which the CBOE currently lists stock options. Blue-chip stocks are shares of common stock in a nationally known company that has a long history of profit growth and dividend payments. It includes most of the titans of American industry, such as AT&T, Exxon, General Motors, and IBM.

The S&P 100 is a value-weighted index. This means that both the price and number of shares outstanding are used to compute the index. Therefore, stocks with large market capitalizations (market price of the stock times the number of shares owned by the stockholders) influence value-weighted indexes most.

To compute the S&P 100, the current market price of each stock in the index is multiplied by the stock's number of outstanding (owned by the stockholders) shares. The resulting market values are then added to determine the total market value of the stocks in the index. The current value of the S&P 100 Index is computed by dividing the total market value by the base value and multiplying by 100. The S&P 100 base value initially was determined by the aggregate market value of the 100 stocks as of January 2, 1976. Base values for the S&P 100 Index are adjusted over time to reflect changes in capitalization that result from mergers, acquisitions, stock rights, splits, and substitutions. The S&P 100 Index is highly correlated with the S&P 500 Index and the Dow Jones Industrial Average (DJIA).

Each index options contract has a value of $100 (the index multiplier) times the current value of the index. For example, if the index is at 465, the underlying dollar value of one index options contract equals $46,500 (465 × $100). An index call gives the holder of the option the right, but not the obligation, to buy $100 times the index value at the exercise price. Ownership of an index options contract confers the right to exercise the option. The S&P 100 option is an American-style option, which means that it can be exercised by the holder at any time prior to expiration.

Since the S&P 100 Index is by far the most widely traded of all index options, an options investor should be aware of its contractual terms. The S&P 100 is traded on the Chicago Board Options Exchange (CBOE), where over 90 percent of all index options contracts are traded. Among the most important terms of the S&P 100 Index options contract are the following:

- *Symbol on the exchange.* OEX
- *Trading unit.* Each index options contract represents $100 (the index multiplier) times the current value of the S&P index. For example, when the index is at 450, the dollar value of a contract will equal $45,000 ($100 × 450).
- *Expiration dates.* S&P 100 Index options expire on a monthly basis in the four nearby months. The final expiration is the Saturday following the third Friday

33

of the expiration month. Investors interested in longer-term options can trade the S&P 500, which has an expiration of up to two years.

- *Premium quotations.* Option premiums are expressed in terms of dollars and fractions per unit of the index. Each point represents $100. As with stock options, the minimum fraction is $\frac{1}{16}$ for option series trading below 3 and $\frac{1}{8}$ for all other series. For example, a premium of $1\frac{3}{16}$ represents $118.75.
- *Exercise prices.* Exercise prices are set at 5-point intervals to bracket the current value of the index. New exercise prices are added when the current value of the index approaches the limits of the existing exercise prices.
- *Aggregate exercise prices.* The aggregate exercise price is the index multiplier ($100) times the exercise price. For example, the aggregate exercise price of a 475 option is $47,500 ($100 × 475).
- *Exercise settlement.* Index options are settled by the payment of cash and not by the delivery of the securities that make up the index. Recall that stock options are settled by the delivery of securities. Upon exercise, the options holder receives a cash amount equal to the difference between the closing dollar value of the index on the exercise date and the aggregate exercise price of the option.

S&P 500 and MMI. The CBOE also offers S&P 500 index options, which were introduced in 1983. These options are based upon the 500 stocks in the S&P 500 Composite Index. The S&P 500 is the most widely followed barometer of stock market movements after the DJIA. It is made up of 400 industrial, 20 transportation, 40 utility, and 40 financial stocks. The index consists primarily of NYSE-listed companies, but it also includes some AMEX and over-the-counter stocks. Like the S&P 100 Index, it is a value-weighted series. However, options based on this series differ from S&P 100 options in that the S&P 500 options are European-style options. European-style options can be exercised only at expiration.

The third major type of index option are those based on the American Stock Exchange Major Market Index (MMI), a price-weighted index of twenty blue-chip stocks that are listed on the NYSE. "Price-weighted" means that the component stock prices are added together and the result is divided by another figure, the divisor. As a result, a high-priced stock has a greater effect on the index than a low-priced stock.

Since fifteen of the twenty MMI stocks are included in the DJIA, this index closely mimics movements of the DJIA. A 1-point movement in this index approximates a 5-point move in the DJIA. Dow Jones & Company has refused to give permission to list options based upon the Dow Jones averages.

15

RISK

Listed stock options have the proven ability to help investors control the risks and rewards of investing in individual common stocks. But what is missing with listed stock options for many investors is the ability to fully hedge against the risk or profit from movements in the overall market.

Although individual stocks are affected by movements in the overall market, some stocks tend to be less volatile than the market as a whole, while others exceed the volatility of the overall market, and a few may even move in a direction that is contrary to the market.

Stock index options were designed to fill the need that stock options could not fully satisfy. They enable investors who have opinions about movements in the overall market to hedge against market risk or to profit from movements in the market. Stock index options are, by far, the most actively traded options.

One way to examine risk is to divide it into three components:

- market risk
- industry risk
- firm-specific risk

Market, or systematic, risk is the risk that results from movements in the overall market. Market risk affects every stock to some extent. It results from economic factors such as changes in interest rates, inflationary expectations, global investment flows, and consumption spending. Studies have shown that the market component of individual stock risk can be as high as 50 percent.

Industry risk is caused by developments unique to the industry in which a firm operates. Examples of industry risk include foreign competition, changes in the regulatory environment in which the industry operates, and product obsolescence. Industry risk tends to be less of a factor in overall risk than market risk.

Firm-specific risk results from factors peculiar to an individual company. Examples include the departure of key management personnel, strikes, ability to maintain quality, and the development of new products.

Diversification can substantially reduce industry risk and firm-specific risk. Diversification is the spreading of risk by allocating funds to a variety of investments. However, diversification cannot significantly reduce market risk. All stock prices move more or less in tandem with the general market. A substantial portion of stock price volatility and nearly all the risk associated with a well-diversified portfolio is market risk.

16

USING INDEX OPTIONS

Let's consider some basic options strategies an investor might employ. Assume that an investor anticipates a rise in the market and decides to buy call options to profit from the market's appreciation.

EXAMPLE:
Suppose that on July 1, the S&P 100 Index closed at 485.00. An investor who buys three September 490 call options at a premium of 12 pays $3,600 (each point on the index represents $100). The market rallies by August with the index standing at 500, and the investor decides to sell at a premium of 15. The investor's profit would be $2,100, computed as follows:

Selling price of 15 × 3 calls × $100	$4,500
Buying price of 12 × 3 calls × $100	3,600
Profit	$ 900

The investor makes a return of 37.5 percent (900/2,400) on a $2,400 investment. Meanwhile, the index rose from 485.00 to 500.00, which represents a 3.1 percent increase. If the index had decreased in value, the maximum loss would be the premium of $3,600, because the maximum loss of any option purchase is always defined by the premiums paid.

As mentioned previously, stock index options are effective tools for hedging strategies. Suppose that an investor of a well-diversified portfolio concludes that the market is about to have a short-term drop. A portfolio that is well-diversified is largely insulated from firm-specific and industry risk. However, market risk cannot be diversified away. Several strategies can be used to hedge against portfolio risk. For example, an investor could choose to sell calls. The sale of calls would hedge market risk to the extent of premiums received from writing the options. The premium could offset some of the downside risk from a general market decline. The risk is the possibility that the index may increase beyond the sum of the exercise price and the premium. In that case, the loss on the options position could exceed the gains on the portfolio.

Another way an investor can hedge a diversified portfolio is to buy index puts. If the market declines, the decrease in the portfolio's value would be at least partially offset by an increase in the value of the puts. The maximum possible loss on this trade would be the premium on the puts.

An investor can provide a portfolio approximate coverage by dividing the portfolio value by the current index times $100 (index multiplier). This is the number of contracts that equates to the stock portfolio. For a portfolio of $600,000, when the S&P 100 Index is 500, 12 contracts ($600,000 / (500 × $100)) would provide approximate coverage. This number may not be a totally accurate hedge, since the stock portfolio can change in value to a different extent than the stock index.

In a declining market, the puts will produce profits to offset the losses on the stock portfolio. If the market rises, the options position will show losses offsetting appreciation in the stock portfolio. The hedged position should be generally stable in value until the hedge is liquidated.

17

OPTIONS ON INTEREST RATES

Few factors affect stocks, mutual funds, real estate, and fixed-income instruments more than interest rates. Interest rates are a constant topic of discussion in the financial media. The most closely watched interest rates are the rates on Treasury bills, notes, and bonds. Treasury bills, the recognized benchmark of short-term interest rates, mature in less than one year. Treasury notes mature between one and ten years, whereas Treasury bonds mature and repay their face value within a period of ten to thirty years from the date of issue.

Although options on Treasury securities are available, it is also possible to speculate directly on interest rates. No investor should underestimate the difficulty in predicting trends in interest rates. Interest rates reflect changes in the economy, inflationary expectations, and the value of the U.S. dollar. Even economists seldom agree on the future course of interest rates.

The Chicago Board Options Exchange (CBOE) has issued four types of options on interest rates: an option based upon the current rate of the most recently auctioned 13-week Treasury bill (IRX), an option based upon the yield-to-maturity on the most recently auctioned 5-year Treasury note (FVX), an option based upon the 10-year Treasury note (TNX), and an option based upon the 30-year Treasury bond (TYX). All of these options are based upon an underlying value (called a composite) that is calculated using interest rates rather than the price of Treasury bonds or bills. When interest rates rise, the value of the underlying call option tends to rise, whereas a decline in interest rates increases the value of the underlying put option.

The values of all of the composites are 10 times the underlying Treasury rates. For example, an annualized yield of 6.0 percent on newly auctioned 13-week Treasury bills would place the composite at 60.00. An average yield-to-maturity on the underlying 30-year Treasury bonds of 8.75 percent would place the composite at 87.50. The values of the composites change as Treasury rates change. For example, if the Treasury bill composite stood at 80.00 and short-term rates rose to 8.50 percent, the Treasury bill composite value would increase to 85.00. For every percentage-point change in interest rates, the interest rate composites change 10 points. All of these options trade on an exchange regulated by the Securities and Exchange Commission. As with other exchange-listed options, investors can buy or sell both puts and calls. Like all listed options, these options offer public bid/ask prices, last-sale information, and an exchange floor with traders obligated to make markets.

18

THE 90/10 STRATEGY

The 90/10 strategy involves purchasing calls on the same number of shares of stock that would have been purchased outright and investing the difference in a fixed-income security such as Treasury bills. The name of the strategy derives from the most common proportion in which the assets are allocated: 90 percent in Treasury bills and 10 percent in index call options.

This strategy is particularly appropriate for an investor who is not interested in individual stock selection and who wishes to participate in the growth of the stock market with limited risk. Interest on the Treasury bills typically covers about one-third of the possible loss on the calls. This strategy permits the investor to benefit from a favorable stock price move while limiting the downside risk to the call premium less any interest earned. It is a particularly effective approach in periods of high interest rates.

EXAMPLE:

Assume that the common stock of XYZ sells at $40 per share. The purchase of 100 shares would cost $4,000. The $4,000 represents the maximum amount that can be invested.

The alternative would be to use the 90/10 strategy. An index call option would be purchased with an exercise price of $40 per share. If the premium is $4 per share, the cost of the option would be $400. This approach leaves the investor with $3,600 that can be invested in Treasury bills.

Suppose the Treasury bills mature in six months and earn 6 percent interest. The $3,600 would earn interest of $108 ($3,600 × .06 × 6/12). This interest reduces the investor's cost of the call to $292 ($400 minus $108).

The $292 also represents the investor's maximum risk exposure compared to the $4,000 cost if the 100 shares were purchased outright.

The beauty of this strategy is that although the risk is limited, the potential capital appreciation is not. Once the market price of XYZ increases by $1.08, the call buyer should realize the same dollar appreciation at expiration as that of an investor who owns 100 shares of the common stock. Therefore, this strategy limits risk to the net cost of the call while still enabling investors to realize capital appreciation.

19

STRADDLES

A straddle is the simultaneous purchase of a put and a call on the same stock, with the identical exercise price and expiration month. Typically, the buyer of a straddle anticipates a substantial movement in a stock but is uncertain what the direction will be. Since the investor is betting on an extraordinary stock movement, the odds are good that he/she will lose. Hence, this strategy is risky and should be undertaken only by experienced options traders.

The buyer of a straddle risks losing only the amount of the premium. The maximum loss occurs only if the price of the stock on the expiration date of the options is exactly equal to the exercise price. Although it is difficult to lose the entire premium paid for a straddle, it can also be difficult to make a profit. Either the put or the call side of a straddle is almost certain to expire worthless. As a result, the stock has to move substantially for a profit to be made.

EXAMPLE:

Suppose that an investor purchases both a put and a call on a stock, paying $5 for the call and $4 for the put, for a total of $9. Also suppose that the underlying stock's price is $60 and that the exercise price of the options is $60. If the price of the stock rises above $69 or drops below $51, the investor will make a profit. Only if the stock expires at the exercise price of $60 will the investor lose his/her entire investment. The investor loses only part of his/ her investment at any other price between $51 and $69.

A profit is earned by the investor only if the stock sells at a price exceeding $69 or drops to less than $51. If the stock rises to $75 and the investor exercises his/her call at

$60, the investor's profit is $6 ($15 – $9 premium). Alternatively, if the stock drops to $43 per share and the investor exercises his/her put at $60, his/her profit is $8 ($17 – $9 premium). Thus, the investor is assured of a profit only if the stock moves by more than $9 in either direction.

One of the most profitable strategies options traders can undertake is straddle writing. This options maneuver involves the issuance of both a put and a call on the same underlying stock when the exercise prices and the expiration dates of the put and the call are identical.

Conservative investors who write straddles use a covered writing strategy. In other words, straddles are backed by stock ownership in the event the call portion of the straddle is exercised. In addition, they have sufficient funds to pay for any shares they could be forced to buy as a result of the call's being exercised.

In flat or unchanging markets, time works against the straddle buyer and in favor of the straddle writer. The straddle writer's profits rise as maturity approaches because of the decay in time value. The significant weakness of covered straddle writing is that the price of the stock may decline sharply. Every dollar that the stock declines below the exercise price reduces the value of the investor's position by one dollar on the stock he/she owns and one dollar on the stock that will be sold to him/her by the owner of the put side of the straddle. Using the above example, the writer of the straddle will earn a profit as long as the price of the stock involved stays between $51 and $69.

20

SPREADS

A spread is the purchase and sale of options on the same underlying stock. The options may be either at the same exercise price with different expiration months, or at different exercise prices with the same or different expiration months. It is a sophisticated strategy aimed at reducing the risk associated with a simple long (opening buy) or short (opening sale) transaction, and should be used only by experienced traders.

There are two basic types of spreads: bull and bear. A *bull spread* involves the purchase of an option with a lower exercise price, and the sale of an option with a higher exercise price. In a *bear spread,* the option with a lower exercise price is sold, and the option with a higher exercise price is bought. A bull spread is most profitable when the underlying stock's value increases, whereas a bear spread is most profitable when the underlying stock's value falls.

The simplest way to execute a bull spread is to purchase an at-the-money call option and sell an out-of-the-money call option. Both options have the same time to maturity but different exercise prices. The lower-priced option is purchased in the hope that the underlying stock will increase in value between the time of purchase and expiration. If that happens, the long-in-the-money option will increase in value at a faster rate than the higher, short position.

For an investor who is confident that the market is going to rise substantially, purchasing calls would be a better strategy. However, a bull spread is less risky than a simple long position because the cost of the long position is reduced by the amount received from the sale of the call option.

EXAMPLE:

A trader buys one October 40 XYZ call and sells one October 45 XYZ call when the underlying stock is priced at $39. If the stock rises to $44, the October 40 call will rise point for point with the underlying stock because it is in the money. The call sold will not increase in value to the same extent because it is still out of the money. The trader could close this position at a profit.

A trader who wants to profit from a declining market and limit risk can engage in a bear spread. The simplest way to accomplish a bear spread is to purchase an at-the-money put option and sell an out-of-the-money put option. In a bear spread, both put options have the same time to maturity but different exercise prices.

EXAMPLE:

A trader buys one October 40 XYZ put and sells one October 35 XYZ put when the underlying stock is $41 per share. If the stock drops to $37, the October 40 put purchased will rise point for point with the drop in the underlying stock, because it is in the money. The put sold will not increase in value to the same extent, because it is still out of the money. The trader could close this position at a profit.

21

LEAPS

Introduced in 1990, Long-term Equity AnticiPation Securities (LEAPS) are options on individual stocks that provide the owner the right to purchase or sell shares of a stock at a specified price on or before a given date up to three years in the future. In contrast, short-term options have an expiration time of nine months.

Since their introduction, LEAPS have grown rapidly in popularity, particularly among individual investors. In 1994, the Chicago Board Options Exchange (CBOE) estimated that more than half of all outstanding LEAPS options contracts were held by individual investors.

LEAPS are available in 1995 on more than 150 securities and several financial indexes and you can expect this list to continue growing as they continue to increase in popularity. Currently, five U.S. exchanges trade these options: the Chicago Board Options Exchange (CBOE), the American Stock Exchange (AMEX), the Philadelphia Stock Exchange (PHLX), the Pacific Stock Exchange (PSE), and the New York Stock Exchange (NYSE).

LEAPS are available in two types: calls and puts. A call gives its holder the right to buy an underlying number of shares, whereas a put gives its holder the right to sell a set number of shares. The owner of a call has the right during the three-year period but not the obligation to purchase the underlying interest, although sellers are obligated to make this sale should the buyer exercise this right. The owner of a put is not obligated to make the sale, although sellers are obligated to buy the underlying interest should the owner exercise the option.

LEAPS options can be effective vehicles for either hedging or speculating. LEAPS calls provide those investors with a longer term view of the stock market an opportunity to benefit from increases in the prices of stocks at a substantially lower price than required to purchase stock. Should a stock appreciate over the three-year term to a level above the exercise price of the LEAPS, an investor could sell his LEAPS contracts in the open market for a profit providing the sales price including commissions exceeded the total price paid. As with any option, LEAPS may expire worthless and may fluctuate more than the price of the underlying stock.

LEAPS can also be used to reduce the downside risk of a stock investment. The purchase of a LEAPS put gives the holder the right to sell the underlying stock at the strike price for the life of the option. Index LEAPS options can be effectively used by investors who would like to hedge several stocks in a given industry segment or even their entire portfolio.

LEAPS vs. Short-term Options. The cost of a typical LEAPS is higher than the cost of a short-term option. However, the higher LEAPS cost is offset by the longer time to expiration. The General Electric January 1996 LEAPS call option price on February 22, 1995 for a strike price of $55 was $4, whereas a short-term option expiring in June 1995 was 2¼ for the same strike price. General Electric was selling for $55⅛ on February 22, 1995. The LEAPS price was 1.8 times higher than the short-term option, but the time to expiration for the LEAPS option is 2.8 times greater than the short-term option. On a daily basis, the LEAPS call costs 1.4 cents per share, whereas a short-term option costs 1.9 cents per share (see Exhibit 2).

Although LEAPS will always trade at a higher price than an identical short-term option, the important advantage for LEAPS is that the time value of a new LEAPS is considerably less sensitive to the daily changes in the time to expiration than is a new short-term option. Thus, a LEAPS investor loses less time value for each day the option is held than a short-term option holder. This price advantage applies to both calls and puts. Once a LEAPS option's time to expiration is similar to a short-term option, its price pattern will duplicate that of a short-term option as it moves toward expiration.

Index LEAPS. Many investors use options based upon their belief in movements of the market as a whole rather than anticipating individual stock price movement. Index LEAPS give the investor the ability to create a long-term position in an option that has the same investment horizon as the investor's market position. There are more than ten different index LEAPS ranging from the S&P 500 and S&P 100 to market indexes like Mexico and Japan.

S&P Index LEAPS are based upon one-tenth the value of the S&P 500 (SPX) or S&P 100 (OEX). The Index LEAPS provide the investor with the ability to control market exposure in finer increments because they represent options with considerably smaller underlying values than full-size, shorter-term index options. If OEX is at 450.00, representing an underlying value of $45,000 (450.00 × $100), the OEX LEAPS would be based upon a price of 45.00, representing an underlying value of $4,500 (45.00 × $100).

Contract Dates. Unlike shorter-term options, all LEAPS options expire in January. Short-term options are assigned to one of three cycles: the January (April, July, October) cycle, the February (May, August, November) cycle, or the March (June, September, December) cycle. At any point in time, a short-term option will have contracts with four expiration dates outstanding, the two near-term months and two-further term months. Expiration for both LEAPS and short-term options occurs on the Saturday following the third Friday of the expiration month.

Further information on LEAPS can be obtained by contacting the CBOE (1-800-843-2639).

EXHIBIT 2
Time-Value Cost of GE LEAPS vs. GE Short-term Options*

Option Type	Strike Price ($)	Premium ($)	No. of Days to Expiration	Cost per Day/per Share (¢)
LEAPS Call	55	4.00	318	1.4
Short-term Call	55	2.25	115	1.9

*GE common stock was selling for $55⅛ on February 22, 1995.

22

TIPS ON BUYING OPTIONS

Options are an exciting part of the investment arena and continue to attract much interest. In 1993, on the CBOE, 79.7 million calls and 60.6 million puts were traded for a total of 140,348,955 contracts, up 15.54 percent from 1992. It's easy to see why options are so attractive to investors.

The returns can be many times the option's cost if the buyer anticipates the market correctly. But although buyers may win big, they don't win often. Three conditions make it difficult to generate profit consistently:

1. Options lose value as the expiration date approaches.
2. About a third of all options expire worthless.
3. Option transaction costs are high (7 to 10 percent of the amount invested).

With options, investors not only have to be right, but right within a limited time frame. Studies have shown that most of the moneymakers in options are those who sell (write) them. Although the returns on writing calls are not extraordinary, they are consistent.

However, if an investor realizes that options are not an easy road to riches, adopts a consistent, disciplined approach, and follows some basic rules, options can be profitable investments. These basic rules include:

1. *Make it simple.* Don't adopt complicated strategies you don't fully understand. Focus upon a few of the more widely used strategies.
2. *Be safe.* Never risk more than you can afford to lose.

3. *Choose a reasonable expiration period.* As a rule, options with more than six months to expiration should be avoided. They're more expensive and, since they are not actively traded, they are illiquid. Options that expire in a few weeks should also be avoided. Remember that the time value of an option declines very little in the early days of its life, but rapidly shrinks toward zero in the last six weeks before expiration.

4. *Avoid options that have too much or too little intrinsic value.* In-the-money options have intrinsic value and sell for a relatively higher premium. Out-of-the-money options have no intrinsic value and, therefore, sell for a lower premium. Investors should avoid deep-in-the-money options, which are expensive and have limited profit potential. Alternatively, although deep-out-of-the-money options may be tempting because the premiums are so low, only an extraordinary move can make these options profitable. Generally speaking, investors should confine themselves to slightly out-of-the-money, slightly in-the-money, or at-the-money options.

5. *Diversification is absolutely necessary.* Don't put all your eggs in one basket. If you buy stock options, you should have at least three options positions on different stocks. Don't concentrate exclusively on calls, as do many investors who have a bullish orientation. Hedge your portfolio of stocks and/or call options by buying puts on one of the stock index contracts. An appropriate hedge would be between a third and a half of portfolio value.

6. *A partial writing strategy against existing stock positions is an excellent defensive strategy.* If you own 1,000 shares of stock, sell 4 to 6 calls against the position. This strategy provides you with cash flow and downside protection, while maintaining upward potential.

7. *Don't sell uncovered (naked) options.* The risk of an options buyer is limited to the premium. Options

sellers (writers) who do not have a position in the underlying stock face unlimited risk. The premium received does not justify this risk.

8. *Have a plan.* Select a target price at the time you establish an options position, and don't deviate from it. Remember that you can enter your sell orders at the target price in advance. You should sell anytime your investment doubles.

23

SELECTING
A BROKER

Options can be traded only through a registered broker or dealer. Although brokers and dealers are closely regulated by the SEC, it is important to be careful in selecting one. A broker should be both knowledgeable about the market and effective in meeting the needs of clients. This includes handling purchase and sale orders, offering appropriate advice and research material about stocks, monitoring accounts to ensure there are no clerical errors, and seeing that money owed to customers is promptly mailed.

There are three main types of brokers: full-service, discount, and deep-discount. *Full-service brokers* provide recommendations and offer advice to their clients. Most of these brokers are members of firms that contain research departments. Some of the largest ones are Merrill Lynch, Prudential Securities, Dean Witter, PaineWebber, and Shearson Lehman.

Discount brokers appeal to investors who do their own research, know precisely what they want, and can make their own buy-and-sell decisions. Investors can save between 30 and 70 percent on their commissions by using a discount broker. Discount brokers simply execute orders, employing salaried order clerks who do not receive commissions. They also provide routine services. Examples of discount brokers are Charles Schwab, Quick & Reilly, and Muriel Sielbert.

Deep-discount brokers change investors about half the rate of a discount broker, and a quarter the rate of full-service brokers on most trades. These firms are principally bare-bones order takers. They are often used by stock market experts, who know what they want and don't need advice. Examples of deep-discount brokers include National Discount Brokers, Brown & Co., and Waterhouse Securities.

Opening an account with a brokerage firm is similar in some respects to opening a bank account. A prospective investor must provide his or her name, address, occupation, social security number, citizenship, proof of age, and a bank or financial reference. However, if the account is to trade on listed options, information on income, net worth, and investment experience is required. In addition, the prospective investor must acknowledge receipt of a current Options Clearing Corporation prospectus and sign an "options agreement" verifying the data on the account form.

An investor who decides to trade options must first contact a broker and ask for a quote. The quote consists of two numbers: the bid price (the highest price anyone is willing to pay) and the asked price (the lowest price at which anyone is willing to sell). The investor can choose among several types of orders:

1. *Market order.* The investor receives the best price available when the order is executed. Market orders are used by investors who want to establish option positions or get out of existing option positions. Investors who enter market orders are often disappointed at the executed price. To avoid these situations, all the exchanges permit investors to place limit orders.

2. *Limit order.* A limit order stipulates that an options trade can be executed only at a specific price.

3. *Stop order.* A stop order is a very effective tool for preventing an investor from becoming too emotionally attached to a position. A stop order to sell becomes a market order when an option sells at or below the stop price (premium). A stop order to buy becomes a market order when an option sells at or above the stop price. For example, suppose you buy 10 XYZ January 35 call options at a premium of 5. To protect at least part of your investment, you instruct your broker to enter a sell stop order for the options

at 3. Should the options drop to 3, the sell stop order is converted into a market order to sell at the best price currently available.

All orders are *day orders* unless otherwise indicated. A day order is good for the day of entry only. An investor can also choose to place a "good until canceled order," which means that the order remains in effect until executed or canceled.

Some brokers claim to be experts in options when in fact they are not. A broker who has not specialized in trading options for at least three years is not experienced in trading options. Brokers are anxious to handle options trades for two reasons:

1. The commissions on options are much higher than are commissions on common stock trades.
2. Options trading involves much more activity than trading in common stocks. Most listed options expire within nine months, and many of the more popular options expire even more quickly. In addition, options traders turn their money over much faster than do stock traders. Investors who buy common stocks or bonds may hold them for years.

Therefore, don't just accept a broker's word that he or she is knowledgeable about options. Start by finding out who the firm's specialists are. Then arrange for an interview with one of them. This interview should not be conducted during trading hours, when the broker may be busy and distracted. Prepare a list of questions concerning both the options market and the broker's experience in options trading.

Another tip in dealing with full-service brokerage firms involves commissions. Don't necessarily accept the list price. Since 1975, commissions have been negotiable. And most major brokerage firms now permit their brokers to grant discounts. In many cases, discounts are pegged to the client's volume of business.

24

INFORMATION ON OPTIONS

It should be stated again that options are not for casual investors. To make money trading options, an investor must work hard and study. Options positions have to be carefully selected and constantly monitored. Before allocating capital to options, investors should test their ideas on paper.

Fortunately, there is a large amount of information available to assist investors in becoming successful options traders. Good starting points are the exchanges that trade options. All the exchanges provide packets of information, usually at no charge. Investors can contact the exchanges at the following addresses:

American Stock Exchange
Options Marketing Department
86 Trinity Place
New York, NY 10006
1-800-THE-AMEX
1-800-462-AMEX (within New York)

Chicago Board Options Exchange
LaSalle at Van Buren
Chicago, IL 60605
1-800-OPTIONS

New York Stock Exchange
Options and Index Products
20 Broad Street
New York, NY 10005
1-800-692-6973

Pacific Stock Exchange
Options Marketing
220 Montgomery #201
San Francisco, CA 94104
1-800-TALK-PSE

Philadelphia Stock Exchange
1900 Market Street
Philadelphia, PA 19103
1-800-THE-PHLX

Barron's is a weekly financial publication that provides an indispensable source of statistical data on all securities as well as options and futures. The *Barron's* options statistics are the most complete found anywhere. Its listings include useful information that is not available in daily newspapers. For example, *Barron's* provides information on "open interest," which indicates the number of options outstanding. An option's open interest expands as new positions are assumed and contracts as positions are closed. Therefore, it is a measure of liquidity and provides a trader an indication of the relative ease of moving in and out of a particular option.

In addition, *Barron's* includes an excellent column in each issue titled "The Striking Price." Written by Thomas N. Cochran, the column is a useful source of information on options trading. Although the column makes no specific recommendations, it reports the recommendations of other brokers and traders. *Barron's* costs $135 for a one-year subscription and can be purchased by contacting:

Barron's
200 Burnett Road
Chicopee, MA 01020
1-800-228-6262

Subscribers should also request a copy of the educational edition as well as the booklet entitled *The ABC's of Options Trading,* offered free of charge.

Probably the best single book devoted to options trading is *The Options Manual,* by Gary Gastineau (McGraw-Hill, 3rd ed., 1988). Suitable for both beginners and seasoned traders, the book is a comprehensive discussion of all aspects of options trading. It is particularly instructive in evaluation of an options contract and the impact of options on the risk-return characteristics of a portfolio.

For beginners, a good introduction is provided by *Getting Started in Options,* by Michael Thomsett (Wiley, 2nd ed., 1993). The book's focus is upon trading individual equity options and it provides a good introduction to various strategies that can be employed.

25

FUTURES

The most risky and speculative of all the markets in the investment arena is the futures market. A futures contract is an agreement between two parties that commits one party to sell a commodity or security to the other at a given price and on a specified future date. Futures contracts are based upon an ever-expanding list of commodities that today includes agricultural products, metals, petroleum, financial instruments, foreign currencies, and stock indexes. In addition, this market now includes options on futures contracts, which enable options buyers to participate in futures markets with predetermined risks.

Futures make it possible to transfer risk from those who want to avoid it (hedgers) to those who are willing to accept it (speculators). Hedgers are individuals or firms that make purchases and sales in the futures market solely for the purpose of establishing a price level—weeks or months in advance—for something they later intend to buy or sell in the cash market. Their purpose is to protect themselves against the risk of an unfavorable price change in the interim.

The first organized commodity exchange in the United States was the Chicago Board of Trade (CBOT), founded in Chicago in 1848. This exchange was originally intended as a central market for the conduct of cash grain business, and it was not until 1865 that the first futures transaction was performed there. Today, the Chicago Board of Trade, with over 41 percent of all contracts traded in the United States, is the largest futures exchange in the world.

Financial futures were not introduced until the 1970s. In 1976, the International Monetary Market (IMM), a subsidiary of the Chicago Mercantile Exchange (CME), began the 90-day Treasury bill futures contract. The following year, the CBOT initiated the Treasury bond futures contract. In 1981, the IMM created the Eurodollar futures contract.

A major financial futures milestone was reached in 1982, when the Kansas City Board of Trade introduced a stock index futures contract based upon the Value Line Stock Index. This offering was followed in short order by the introduction of the S&P 500 Index futures contract on the Chicago Mercantile Exchange and the New York Stock Exchange Composite Index traded on the New York Futures Exchange. All of these contracts provide for cash delivery rather than delivery of securities.

Trading volume on the futures exchanges has surged in the last three decades—from 3.9 million contracts in 1960 to 426.3 million contracts in 1994. In their short history, financial futures have become the dominant factor in the futures markets. In 1994, 65 percent of all futures contracts traded were financial futures. The most actively traded futures contract is the Eurodollar contract traded on the CME.

Trading in futures is regulated by the Commodity Futures Trading Commission (CFTC), an independent federal agency consisting of five commissioners appointed by the President. The CFTC serves principally an oversight role by determining that self-regulation is continuous and effective.

The National Futures Association (NFA), formed in 1982, is a congressionally authorized self-regulatory organization that is subject to CFTC oversight. It polices activities of both exchange member firms and nonmember firms throughout the futures industry. In addition, the NFA has the responsibility for registering persons and firms that are required to be registered with the CFTC.

It is against the law for any person or firm to offer futures contracts for purchase or sale unless those contracts are traded on one of the nation's regulated futures exchanges and the person or firm is registered with the CFTC. In addition, persons and firms conducting futures-related business with the public must be NFA members. Therefore, you should be extremely cautious if approached by a party attempting to sell you a futures-related investment unless you are able to verify that the party is registered with the CFTC and is an NFA member. You can quickly do this verification by phoning the NFA toll-free at 800-621-3570.

Futures are often confused with options, but there are important differences between the two types of instruments. An option permits the buyer to choose whether or not to exercise the option by a specified date. In other words, with an option, the buyer purchases a right, and only the writer takes on an obligation. On the other hand, with futures, both sides take on an obligation. A futures contract obligates the buyer to buy and the seller to sell at the agreed-upon price on the agreed-upon date.

In addition, the buyer of an option pays a premium to acquire the option. In a futures transaction, neither party pays a premium. Both parties must put up a good-faith deposit to guarantee fulfillment of the purchase or sale obligation. This good-faith deposit is called *margin*.

Futures trading is the riskiest sector of the investment arena. Even successful traders lose money on more than half of their trades. The key to their success lies in cutting their losses short on their losing trades and staying with the profitable trades long enough to more than offset all the small losses. This feature of futures is one reason speculators with less than $20,000 in their accounts are seldom successful. The accounts are not large enough to withstand a series of small losses. Studies have shown that the size of a trading account is related to success in futures trading. Investors with small amounts of capital should avoid this market altogether. Those investors with considerable resources should limit their exposure to no more than 5 to 10 percent of their capital.

Only 1 to 2 percent of all futures contracts actually result in delivery. Very few speculators have the desire to take delivery of 5,000 bushels of corn, 60,000 pounds of soybean oil, or even $100,000 of Treasury notes. As a result, gains and losses are generally realized by buying or selling offsetting futures contracts prior to the delivery date. If delivery does occur, it takes the form of a negotiable instrument such as a warehouse receipt that proves the holder's ownership of the commodity.

The sale of a contract that was previously purchased liquidates a futures contract in the same way that the sale of 100 shares of GM liquidates an earlier purchase of 100 shares of GM. In a similar vein, a futures contract that was initially sold can be liquidated by an offsetting purchase. In any event, gain or loss is computed by taking the difference between the buying price and the selling price.

Cash-settlement futures contracts are contracts that are settled in cash rather than by delivery at the time the contract expires. For example, stock index futures are settled in cash based upon the index number at the close of the final day of trading. No provision exists for delivery of the shares of stock that make up the index.

After the closing bell signals the end of a day's trading, the exchange's clearing organization matches each purchase made that day with the corresponding sale and computes each member firm's gains and losses based upon that day's price changes. The system of daily settlement in the futures markets is called market to market and is conducted through an intermediary body called the futures clearinghouse. Each firm then computes the gains and losses for each of its customers having futures contracts.

Gains and losses on futures contracts are credited and deducted on a daily basis. For example, a $1,000 profit resulting from the day's price changes is immediately credited to the trader's account, and could be withdrawn. Alternatively, a $500 loss resulting from the day's price changes would be immediately debited to the customer's account for that amount. This daily cash settlement is a significant feature of futures trading.

Long vs. Short. The buyer of a futures contract (unless he/she is buying to offset and thus close out an existing short position) is said to be long, or has a long position. The seller of a futures contract (unless he/she is closing out a long position) is said to be short, or has a short position. A speculator sells a futures contract short because he/she believes the market is headed lower and he/she will be able to buy the futures contract back later at a lower price.

In futures, there is a short position for every long position. If an investor buys a futures contract, another market participant must sell it to him/her. If an investor sells a futures contract short, another investor must buy it. Gains on one side of a futures contract must be counterbalanced by losses on the other side of the position. Like options, futures are a zero-sum game. When the longs win, the shorts lose, and vice versa.

26

LEVERAGE

Investors should recognize the extreme risk associated with investing in futures. No other form of investment or speculation is so highly leveraged. An understanding of how leverage magnifies the risks and opportunities associated with the trading of futures is crucial to an understanding of these investment vehicles.

The leverage of futures trading results from the fact that only a relatively small amount of money (known as initial margin) is required to buy or sell a futures contract. For example, a deposit of only $2,000 might enable an investor to buy a futures contract representing $35,000 worth of cotton. The initial margin is typically 5 to 15 percent of the value of the underlying contract, although in some cases it is even less. The smaller the margin in relationship to the value of the futures contract, the greater the leverage and the greater the risk.

High leverage can produce large profits when compared to the initial margin if the speculator correctly anticipates the future price change. Alternatively, if prices move in the opposite direction from what was anticipated, large losses can result. Leverage is a double-edged sword.

EXAMPLE:
Suppose that an investor anticipates rising stock prices and buys one October S&P 500 stock index futures contract at a time when it is trading at 460. The initial margin required is $20,000. Since the value of the S&P futures contract is calculated by multiplying the futures contract by $500, the contract includes $230,000 ($500 × 460) of securities, and each point change in the index represents a $500 gain or loss

Therefore, an increase in the index from 460 to 500 (8.7 percent) would double the investment (40 points × $500 a point), and a decrease from 460 to 420 would wipe out the investment. The 100 percent gain or loss resulted from only an 8.7 percent change in the index. Keep in mind that an 8.7 percent change is equivalent to a 331-point change in the Dow Jones Industrial Average if it stands at 3800, and a 40-point drop in the S&P 500 if it stands at 460. An 8.7 percent change in the index is well within the range of probability.

Although a futures contract provides exactly the same actual profit (dollar amount) as owning or selling short the actual commodities or securities represented by the contract, the low initial margin magnifies the percentage profit or loss potential. In this market, speculators must be prepared for the possibility of losing their investment in a single day. An investor who is not reconciled to that possibility should avoid this market altogether.

27

HEDGING IN FUTURES

Hedging is the fundamental purpose of the futures markets. Many of the rules that govern futures contracts are designed to reflect the hedging needs of commercial interests. Although the details of hedging transactions can be complex, the principle is simple. Hedging involves individuals and firms that make purchases and sales in the futures market to reduce the risk of loss from price fluctuations of the cash asset. The purpose is to protect themselves against the risk of an unfavorable price change in the interim.

The position taken in the futures market is generally opposite and approximately equal to the one held in the cash market. A long position in the futures market—called a "long hedge"—protects against a possible price increase in the commodity (including securities). A long hedge would be used by an individual or firm that is short the actual commodity. For example, an exporter who has promised delivery in several months at an agreed-upon price could engage in a long hedge.

A short position in the futures market—called a "short hedge"—is designed to protect against a possible decrease in the price of the commodity. A short hedge would be executed by a firm or individual who is long the actual commodity. For example, a hog breeder who will bring animals to market in several months is said to be long in the cash market. The breeder could go short (sell futures contracts) in the CME live-hog futures market to protect against the possibility of a decrease in the price of live hogs when they are ready for market.

Hedging techniques are popular with institutional and other professional investors. Stock index futures can be used to hedge a stock portfolio so that the potential for both profits and losses is eliminated. If there is concern about a future market decline, hedging may be preferred to actually selling stocks. The reasons include the following:

1. The tax consequences might be significant.
2. Substantial dividends could be lost.
3. Commission costs may be too high.
4. Uncertainty about the prospect of decline.
5. The decline is expected to be temporary.

To provide a rough-coverage hedge for your portfolio, divide the portfolio value by the current index value times $500. This result is the number of contracts that is equal in value to the stock portfolio. However, this position might not completely hedge a portfolio, because a stock portfolio can change in value to a different degree than the stock index.

EXAMPLE:

Suppose that the manager of a $45 million portfolio is concerned about the short-term market outlook and is willing to give up the potential for gains in order to protect against possible losses. If the index stands at 500, he/she would need to sell 180 contracts ($45 million/(500 × $500)). If the market declines, the gain on the contracts offsets the decline in the portfolio value. If the market rises, the decline in the futures prices offsets the gain on the stock portfolio owned. The hedge can be eliminated at any time by buying back 180 contracts to cancel out those sold.

28

COMMODITY FUTURES

A commodity futures contract is an agreement covering the purchase and sale of physical goods for future delivery on a commodity exchange. The futures contract requires the future seller to deliver to a designated location a specified quantity of a commodity to be sold to the future buyer at a stipulated price on some specified later date. Originally, the purpose of futures was to transfer risk from one party to another and to protect against price fluctuations. Subsequently, speculation has become an important factor in these markets.

Commodity futures are used primarily by four groups of people: producers, consumers, investors, and exchange-floor traders. Producers use the futures market to protect the price they receive for their products. These people range from small farmers to managers of giant companies.

To illustrate, a farmer who thinks the price of corn may decline by harvest time can sell corn futures early in the season. If the price of corn does decline, a profit on the futures will result to compensate for the lower price received for the corn. This transaction is an example of hedging.

Consumers can use futures to protect themselves against a rise in the price of commodities. These consumers can range from food processors to individuals who buy corn or automobiles. To illustrate, a popcorn manufacturer who thinks the price of corn is going to rise and make competing against a maker of potato chips difficult, may buy corn futures for delivery a year later.

If the price of corn rises, the profit on the futures compensates for the higher price paid for the corn. If the price falls, the futures losses are offset by the lower cost of corn. In either case, the popcorn manufacturer has a hedged position that offers protection from fluctuations in the price of corn.

Investors use futures to speculate on future price changes. Theoretically, the speculator assumes the price risk that the hedger is seeking to minimize. When the hedger sells futures, it is the speculator who buys; when the hedger buys futures, it is the speculator who sells. Speculators generally attempt to make short-term profits on a large number of transactions. Typically, the hedger makes a smaller number of transactions and holds each position for a longer period of time. By making it easier for others to buy and sell futures, speculators help to make the market more liquid.

Recently, smaller investors have become more interested in commodity futures. They are lured by the tremendous leverage that investments in commodities provide. Once certain net worth standards are met, only a small deposit, or margin, is required to buy or sell futures. The cash requirement varies from 3 to 15 percent of the contract. For example, $2,000 can buy $35,000 worth of a commodity.

As highly leveraged investments, futures present an opportunity for dramatic profits. However, it is a two-way street: an investor may also incur dramatic losses. A recent study of commodity speculators revealed that 75 percent lose money. Therefore, the risks may outweigh the benefits for many investors.

Exchange-floor traders are another group of commodity futures users. They serve as middlemen by buying from producers and selling to users. As individuals trading for their own or their firm's accounts, these floor traders are an important factor in creating market activity in addition to ensuring that bids and offers are available.

The commodity futures market is very close to being a purely competitive market. There are many buyers and sellers, none of whom is large enough to determine prices. Prices are determined by demand and supply, which are influenced by a variety of forces. These forces involve a range of political, social, and economic factors, in addition to factors peculiar to the particular commodity. Gold is an example of a commodity whose price is strongly influenced by political factors. Prices of most agricultural commodities are determined largely by fluctuations in supply.

Commodity futures markets function primarily as a form of forward pricing (guarantee of a price when delivery of the commodity takes place). Only about 2 percent of all futures contracts actually result in delivery. Typically, futures contracts change hands many times. However, one characteristic supporting the integrity of futures markets is that an investor may actually acquire or deliver a commodity.

29

FINANCIAL FUTURES

Although commodity futures have been traded on exchanges for more than a century, financial futures were not introduced until the 1970s. Financial futures are futures contracts written on securities, money, or stock indexes. Three main types of financial futures are traded: interest rate futures, stock index futures, and currency futures. Unlike commodity futures, financial futures do not involve delivery of a physical property, but rather of financial securities or cash. Like commodity futures, financial futures are used by borrowers, lenders, and other users of financial instruments to hedge their investments.

Investors can use positions in the futures market to protect the gains they have made in the cash market. Speculators can use futures to profit from anticipated changes in interest rates, foreign exchange rates, and movements in the stock market. However, caution is advised to inexperienced investors. All futures markets are dominated by professionals, many of whom employ sophisticated methods to determine their positions. Small investors in these markets don't have a high success rate.

Financial futures are traded on an exchange that has regulations to ensure the performance of contracts. The exchange clearinghouse acts as a third party to and guarantor of all transactions, thus eliminating the need for sellers and buyers to become known to one another. While a future is a commitment to buy or sell at some point in the future, delivery of the underlying instrument rarely occurs. Trades in futures contracts are settled by entering into an offsetting position (a contract sold is closed out by a purchase and a contract bought is closed out by selling the contract).

Although the financial futures market is less than two decades old, about 65 percent of all futures traded in the United States in 1994 were financial futures. Interest-rate futures (e.g., Treasury bills, bonds, and notes) accounted for about 58 percent of all futures trades. In their short existence, financial futures have clearly become the most exciting segment of the futures market.

Limitless hedging opportunities are available in the financial futures market. For example, borrowers can hedge against higher interest rates, and lenders against lower interest rates. Investors can hedge against an overall decline or rise in stock prices. Whatever the strategy, a hedger willingly surrenders the opportunity to benefit from favorable price changes in order to achieve protection against unfavorable price changes.

Speculators are individuals or firms seeking to profit from anticipated increases or decreases in futures prices. Through trading in pursuit of profit, speculators help create a liquid market. An investor "goes long" by purchasing futures contracts in hopes of later selling them at a higher price. On the other hand, an investor "goes short" by selling futures contracts in hopes of later buying back identical and offsetting contracts at a lower price. With futures trading, the investor can profit from declining prices (by selling) or profit from rising prices (by buying).

30

OPTIONS ON FUTURES

In 1982, options on futures were introduced. Recognizing the success of the CBOE and the stock exchanges in trading options, the futures exchanges wanted a piece of the action. Futures options are the financial instruments that permit futures exchanges to also trade options.

A futures option gives the buyer the right—but not the obligation—to buy or sell a particular futures contract at a stated price at any time prior to a specified date. As with ordinary options, there are two distinct types: calls and puts.

The buyer of a call option buys the right—but not the obligation—to purchase a particular futures contract at a stated price at any time during the life of the option. The buyer of a put option acquires the right—but not the obligation—to sell a particular futures contract at a stated price at any time during the life of the option. If the option is exercised, settlement is not in cash but through actual delivery of a futures contract.

Futures options involve two sets of relationships: that between the futures contract and the underlying commodity, security, or index; and that between the option and the futures contract. The additional complication can make futures options even more volatile than regular options. The average options investor should not be assuming this additional risk. These instruments should be traded only by investors familiar with regular options.

Another type of futures option involves Treasury bonds. This type of futures contract is based upon $100,000 face amount of U.S. Treasury bonds. Prices of U.S. bonds and futures are quoted in terms of points and

32nds. Each full point is worth $1,000, and each 32nd is worth $31.25. Thus, a bond with a market value of 99,000 would be quoted at 99-00. A bond quoted at 99-8 (99 and $\frac{8}{32}$) would be worth $99,250. A bond futures contract quoted at 92-04 (92 and $\frac{4}{32}$) would be worth $92,125.

Options on Treasury bond futures contracts are quoted differently from bond and bond futures prices. They are quoted in 64ths of a point. Each 64th is equal to $15.625. Thus, a premium quoted at 3-8 would be 3 points and $\frac{8}{64}$, or $3,125. A premium of 4-32 (4 and $\frac{32}{64}$) would be worth $4,500.

The principal attraction of futures options as opposed to futures is that they offer an options buyer the potential for substantial profit while limiting the buyer's risk to the up-front cost (the premium) of the option. Any options strategy can also be applied to futures options. For example, if interest rates are expected to decline, calls can be purchased or the investor can write (sell) puts to earn the premium. If interest rates are forecasted to rise, puts can be bought or calls can be written to earn the premium. In a stable interest-rate environment, covered calls can be written to earn additional income if cash bonds are held.

31

STOCK INDEX
FUTURES

Stock index futures have enjoyed tremendous growth in trading volume since they were introduced in 1982. A stock index futures contract is a futures contract to buy or sell the face value of a stock index. The two principal stock index futures contracts traded in the United States are the Standard & Poor's (S&P) contract at the Chicago Mercantile Exchange (CME) and the New York Stock Exchange Index contract at the New York Futures Exchange (NYFE). S&P 500 contracts, written on the S&P 500 Index, account for about 90 percent of all stock index futures trading.

The S&P 500 Index is designed to be an accurate proxy for a diversified portfolio of highly capitalized, blue-chip stocks. The index is based upon the stock prices of 500 different companies, including about 400 industrial, 40 utilities, 20 transportation companies, and 40 financial institutions. The market value of the 500 companies is equal to approximately 80 percent of the value of all stocks traded on the New York Stock Exchange (NYSE).

Although the Dow Jones Industrial Average (DJIA) receives greater attention from the media, the S&P is recognized by most professional investors as the benchmark index. Because of its large sample size, its movement is more representative of the stock market as a whole than is the DJIA. The index consists primarily of NYSE-listed companies, but also includes some American Stock Exchange and over-the-counter stocks.

With S&P 500 futures, the commodity is a portfolio of stocks represented by a stock price index. Unlike physical commodities, which may actually be delivered, index futures involve a cash settlement of the difference between the original transaction price and the final price of the index at the termination of the contract.

The value of an S&P futures contract is calculated by multiplying the futures price by $500. For example, with a price of $455.00, the value of the contract would be $227,500 ($500 × 455). The minimum trading price change (called a "tick") for the contract is $.05. Therefore, if the price of the contract goes up a tick from $455.00 to $455.05, the value of the contract increases by $25 ($500 × .05).

The value of the futures price closely follows the value of the index, and the futures price will change as the underlying index changes. However, the price of the future may be higher or lower than the index, depending upon market expectations as to future prices. A summary of S&P 500 contract terms are given below:

Contract:	S&P 500 Index
Size:	$500 × the S&P 500 Stock Price Index
Minimum price change:	05 index points = $25 per contract
Delivery months:	March, June, September, December
Last day of trading:	The Thursday prior to the third Friday of the contract month
Settlement procedure:	Cash settlement

As mentioned before, the futures market is a very fast game. Discipline is an absolute necessity for success. You have to let your profits run, and limit your losses. The leveraged nature of this market makes for stunning changes in your return on the margin you put up.

EXAMPLE:
You are convinced that the market will rise in the next three months. The S&P 500 Index is at 460, and you buy a futures contract at 465 for delivery in three months. The S&P contract represents a value of $500 times the index, for a total of $232,500 ($500 × 465). Assume you

are required to put up margin of $25,000. Each point up or down brings you a return of $500.

Two months later, the index has risen to 473 and your contract is selling for 475. If you decided to sell, your profit would equal ten points, or $5,000. A $5,000 return on $25,000 margin is equal to 20 percent in only two months.

EXAMPLE:
Instead of rising, the contract price dropped to 453 after a month. At this point, you have lost $6,000 (12 points × $500 a point) of the margin you put up. You're likely to get a margin call. Suppose you put up additional margin and the contract price continues to drop to 447. The 18-point drop has wiped out $9,000 of your initial margin of $25,000. The total drop of only 3.9 percent (18 points ÷ 465) cost you 36 percent of your initial margin. Unfortunately, a 3.9-percent drop in the market is very possible, which is why investors in futures should be prepared for these kinds of losses.

32

MARGIN

The term "margin" as applied to common stocks has an altogether different meaning from the same term as applied to futures. Margin on common stock refers to the use of borrowed funds to supplement the investor's own money. The investor makes only partial payment for the securities and borrows the rest. Therefore, trading on margin is essentially trading on credit.

In the futures arena, margin is simply a deposit of good-faith money that can be drawn upon by your brokerage firm to cover losses that may be incurred in the course of futures trading. Both the buyer and the seller of a futures contract have to provide margin. The purpose of margin is to ensure contract performance and the integrity of the marketplace.

Minimum margin requirements for each futures contract are set by the exchange on which the contract is traded. Exchanges can adjust the margin requirements as market conditions and risks change. Also, individual brokerage firms may require margins that are higher than those required by the exchange. Generally, the margin required is about 10 percent of the current value of the futures contract.

Initial margin (sometimes called original margin) is the amount of money that a customer must deposit with a brokerage firm at the time a futures position is established. Depending on exchange requirements, initial margin may consist of cash, funds transferred from another of the customer's accounts, U.S. government securities, a letter of credit, or a negotiable warehouse receipt.

In addition to prescribing minimum margin levels, the exchange sets the maintenance margin requirement. The maintenance margin is the amount of money that must be maintained on deposit while a futures position is open. If profits accrue on an open position, the profits are added to the balance in the margin account. When losses accrue, the losses are deducted from the balance in the margin account.

If the funds in your margin account are reduced by losses to below the maintenance margin requirement, your broker will require you to deposit additional money to bring your account back up to its initial margin. Requests for additional margin are termed *margin calls.* The amount of maintenance margin varies from exchange to exchange, but the 75 percent level is a common standard.

EXAMPLE:

Suppose that the initial margin required to open a futures contract is $2,000 and that the maintenance margin requirement is $1,500. If losses on your open position reduced the balance in your account to $1,450, you would receive a margin call for $550 to restore your account to the initial margin of $2,000.

Futures traders must understand the brokerage firm's margin agreement and know how and when the firm expects margin calls to be met. Delivering margin calls to futures participants is the responsibility of the broker. If a margin call is not met within a suitable period of time, the firm can protect itself by liquidating the investor's open positions at the available market price.

33

ORDERS

Orders to buy or sell futures contracts are either market orders or contingent orders. A *market order* is an order to buy or sell a futures contract at the best possible price as soon as possible. *Contingent orders* include instructions that make their execution dependent upon certain conditions, such as time or price limit.

Each futures order should contain the following items of information:

1. Whether to buy or sell.
2. The number of contracts to be bought or sold.
3. The relevant futures contract, including both delivery month and year.
4. Whether it is a market order or a contingent order.

Although there are many different types of contingent orders, we will discuss only the most important ones. The most common contingent order is a limit order. Limit orders are executed only at a price specified by the customer or at a better price. A limit order to buy may be filled only at or below the limit price, while a limit order to sell may be filled only at or above the limit price. Many investors place limit orders because they are dissatisfied with the prices they receive when they place market orders. However, a limit order provides no assurance of execution. If the limit price is not reached, the order will not be filled.

A *stop order* (sometimes referred to as a *stop loss order*) is an order that becomes a market order when a particular price level is reached. A sell stop is placed below the market and a buy stop is placed above the market. Stop loss orders are used to limit the amount lost if the futures price moves against a position. For example, if you purchased an S&P 500 contract at 460 and wished to limit your possible loss, you might place a stop order to sell an offsetting contract if the price should drop to 440. If the contract price does drop to 440, a stop order becomes an order to execute the trade at the best price currently available.

However, there is no guarantee that it will be possible to execute the order at the price specified in the stop order. In a volatile market, the market price may be declining or rising so rapidly that there is no opportunity to liquidate your position at the stop price designated. The broker's only obligation, under these conditions, is to execute the order at the best price available.

In addition to limiting losses, stop orders can also be used to protect profits. For example, if you have bought S&P 500 futures at 460 and the price is now 490, you might wish to place a stop order to sell if and when the price drops to 480. This order (subject to the previously described limitations of stop orders) could protect most of your profit while still permitting you to gain from any continued increase in price.

34

READING FUTURES PRICES

Exhibit 3 is an example of how futures prices are reported. The second boldfaced line gives the name of the commodity—in this case, corn. Also listed is the exchange, CBT, which stands for the Chicago Board of Trade. Finally, the line lists the size of a single contract (5,000 bushels) and the way in which prices are quoted (cents per bushel).

The first column gives the months in which the delivery of the contract may occur. Trading is usually limited to certain specified months and to less than two years in the future. The next three columns give the opening, highest, and lowest prices of the day. A blank indicates that a particular month hasn't traded that day. The fifth column gives the settlement price, the price brokers use for valuing portfolios and for deciding whether to call for more margin.

The next column, titled "Change," shows the difference between the latest settlement price and the settlement price for the previous day. The second and third columns from the right display the highest and lowest prices at which each contract has been traded. The right-hand column shows the open interest. Open interest is the number of contracts outstanding; it is a measure of the public interest in a contract. The open interest is computed by exchanges after each trading day and reported early the following day.

EXHIBIT 3
Futures Price Quotations

Open Interest Reflects Previous Trading Day.

	Open	High	Low	Settle	Change	Lifetime High	Lifetime Low	Open Interest

—GRAINS AND OILSEEDS—

CORN (CBT) 5,000 bu.; cents per bu.

	Open	High	Low	Settle	Change	Lifetime High	Lifetime Low	Open Interest
Mar	235½	235½	234½	234¾	− ½	282½	220½	17,046
May	242	242¾	241½	242¼	− ¼	285	228	101,303
July	248¼	248½	247½	248	− ¼	285½	232½	93,689
Sept	253¼	253¼	252¼	253	− ¼	270½	238	15,759
Dec	257¼	257¾	256½	257¼	− ½	263	235½	71,176
Mr96	264	264	263¼	264	− ¼	265¾	249½	7,884
May	267¼	267¼	267¼	267¼	− ½	269¼	259½	236
July	269½	269½	268¾	269½	− ½	271½	254	4,004
Dec	256	256½	255½	255½	− ¾	258	239	2,027

Est vol 37,000; vol Wed 36,344; open int 313,173, −2,679.

Source: *The Wall Street Journal.*

To interpret the prices, you have to include the decimal point. For example, a price of 275 means $2.75 a bushel. To calculate a change in the value of your contract caused by a price change, you must take into consideration the contract size. Since the contract size of corn is 5,000 bushels, each point change means $50 (5,000 × .01).

Among the most actively traded futures contracts are those covering Treasury bonds. Treasury bonds, which are Treasury securities maturing in more than ten years, are traded on the Chicago Board of Trade (see Exhibit 4). Underlying the futures contract is $100,000 worth of Treasury bonds. Bonds are quoted in 32nds of one percent of this face value. Thus, a price of 103-12 means 103 and $^{12}/_{32}$ or 103⅜.

For these futures, the lifetime high and low columns are replaced by a column for yields based upon settlement prices and the change in this yield from the previous day. The yield is the interest rate based upon its current price, original interest rate, and remaining life. Since many speculators focus upon interest rates, rather than bond prices, these columns are frequently of greater interest than the prices themselves.

EXHIBIT 4
Futures Price Quotations

—INTEREST RATE—

TREASURY BONDS (CBT)—$100,000; pts. 32nds of 100%

	Open	High	Low	Settle	Chg	Lifetime High	Low	Open Interest
Mar	103–29	104–01	103–04	103–12	–	18116–20	95–13	174,963
June	103–12	103–16	102–18	102–26	–	19113–15	94–27	197,770
Sept	103–00	103–01	102–06	102–12	–	19112–15	94–10	10,040
Dec	102–09	102–15	101–25	101–31	–	19111–23	93–27	732
Mr96	....	....	....	101–19	–	19102–08	93–13	130

Est vol 410,000; vol Wed 515,658; op int 383,714, +1,910.

Source: *The Wall Street Journal.*

35

TECHNICAL ANALYSIS

Two basic approaches exist in forecasting futures prices: technical analysis and fundamental analysis. Fundamental analysis deals with the demand and supply of the physical commodity. Technical analysis is concerned with the study of the action of the futures markets themselves. The key factors of interest to the technical analyst are the level and movement of futures prices, trading volume, and open interest. Most traders use a blend of the two approaches in order to maximize their trading success.

Technical analysis is the attempt to predict future price movements in the futures market by analyzing the way prices have moved in the past. Technical analysts consider such factors as the monetary and fiscal policy of the government, economic environment, industry trends, and political events to be irrelevant in attempting to predict future prices. Their concern is with the historical movement of prices and the effects of supply and demand.

In contrast, the fundamental analyst focuses upon the causes of price movements. In the commodity futures market, for example, the fundamentalist considers the effect of such variables as bumper crops and drought. In financial futures, factors of concern might be the current level of interest rates and trade deficits. In stock options, accounting data are critical to fundamental analysis.

It is a commonly held belief that fundamental analysis is superior to technical analysis in determining long-run trends, while technical analysis is better for predicting shorter trends and timing entry and exit of positions. Although technical analysts acknowledge that prices are ultimately rooted in fundamental factors, they say that it takes too long to process and evaluate supply-and-demand factors. Since technical analysts assume that all influences on market action are automatically accounted for or are discounted in price activity, it is the historical pattern of prices that should be evaluated rather than the many factors that determine supply and demand.

Technical analysts use a wide variety of techniques in attempting to predict futures prices. Many rely upon charts and look for particular configurations that are supposed to have predictive value. Entire books have been devoted to interpreting charts. Another style of technical analysis focuses upon volume, open interest, and the momentum of prices. Others use mechanical trading signals on an automatic basis.

Although the tools and techniques of technical analysis vary greatly, there are certain principles that underlie all forms of technical analysis:

1. Market value is entirely determined by the interaction of demand and supply.
2. Both rational and irrational factors govern demand and supply.
3. Prices tend to show patterns that persist for significant periods of time.
4. Changes in trends are caused by the shift in demand and supply.
5. Chart patterns tend to recur, and can be used to forecast future prices.
6. Shifts in demand and supply can be deduced in charts of market prices.

Although price is the indicator of greatest interest to technical analysts, volume and open interest are important secondary indicators. *Volume* is the number of contracts traded during a specified period of time—usually one day. Every time a trade occurs, volume increases. To determine the volume, sum the total of the short positions taken that day, or add the total of the long positions taken. Do not add the two together, because each contract requires a buyer and a seller.

As a rule, volume is an indicator of the conviction behind a price movement. For example, a continuance of an upward trend is considered more likely when trading volume increases during rallies and dries up during declines. A lack of volume on the upside would mean that the upturn lacks conviction and the market is technically weakening. The opposite would occur in a bear market. In this case, trading volume should tend to increase during declines and slip when prices stage minor rallies.

Open interest is the total number of contracts outstanding or unliquidated at the end of the day. To determine the open interest in a market, add the number of short positions *or* long positions held at the close of the trading day (do not add the two together). Open interest increases when a new long buys from a new short; it decreases when an old long sells to an old short. However, open interest does not change when a new long buys from an old long or a new short sells to an old short. In this case, a new investor is simply replacing the old investor. The following chart summarizes the effect of transactions on open interest:

Buyer	Seller	Change in open interest
Buys new long	Sells new short	Increases
Buys new long	Sells old long	No change
Buys old short	Sells new short	No change
Buys old short	Sells old long	Decreases

Open interest is a valuable diagnostic tool, because it measures the flow of money into the market. Increasing open interest means that money is flowing into the market, and enhances the likelihood that the present trend will continue. A rise in open interest accompanied by rising prices means that buyers are the dominating force in the market. In other words, buyers are more aggressive than the sellers of new shorts. Alternatively, rising open interest combined with weakening prices is an indication that the short sellers are dominating the market and that prices will trend lower. Rising open interest tends to be a confirmation of the existing trend.

A fall in open interest while prices are rallying indicates that short sellers are dominating the market. The rise in prices is largely a reflection of the short sellers' covering their positions. The rise in prices will last only as long as the shorts continue to cover their positions. When the shorts finally stop covering their positions, prices will dip.

A price decline accompanied by falling open interest also suggests a temporary state. This condition suggests that the selling pressure is from the existing longs. Once the existing longs have sold out, prices should rally. The following chart summarizes the interpretation of price, volume, and open interest:

Price	Volume	Open interest	Trend
Rising	Up	Up	Bullish
Rising	Down	Down	Weakening
Declining	Up	Up	Bearish
Declining	Down	Down	Strengthening

These guidelines are not meant to be hard-and-fast rules. Speculating is never that simple. For example, when interpreting open interest, you must consider seasonal factors. In the futures market, open interest is subject to seasonal changes that vary depending upon the nature of the underlying commodity or financial instrument.

Many mechanical trading systems have been developed by technical analysts. In most of these systems, computers are used to process data and generate buy and sell signals. One type of mechanical trading system is the computation of *moving averages*. Moving averages are among the oldest trading tools and are easy to compute. A moving average is an average that is updated by dropping the first number and adding in the last number. The purpose of computing a moving average is to smooth out short-term rises and declines in prices and reveal the underlying trend. For example, suppose that the closing prices for a commodity over three days were 60.50, 60.75, and 60.55.

Day 1	60.50
Day 2	60.75
Day 3	60.55
	$181.80 \div 3 = 60.60$

The average of the three prices is 60.60. Suppose that the price at the close of the fourth day is 60.35. In this case, the new three-day moving average would be computed as follows:

Day 2	60.75
Day 3	60.55
Day 4	60.35
	$181.65 \div 3 = 60.55$

The new three-day moving average is computed by eliminating the first day and adding the next three days together and dividing by 3. The decline in the closing price on the fourth day caused the moving average to fall from 60.60 to 60.55.

Any number of days can be used to compute a simple moving average. The shorter the moving average, the more sensitive it will be to price changes. The longer the number of days selected, the less responsive the average will be to price changes. A simple rule in trading based upon a single moving average is to be long when the daily closing price is above the moving average and short when the daily closing price is below the moving average.

36

FUNDAMENTAL ANALYSIS

With commodities, all significant price moves are rooted in fundamental factors. Unless there is an actual shortage or surplus of the actual commodity, unusually low or high prices cannot be maintained. The aim of fundamental analysis is to recognize a developing imbalance between demand and supply and take a position in the futures market that will profit from the eventual price change this imbalance will cause.

The fundamental analyst estimates the supply of the commodity in the near future, and the demand there will be for it. The supply of a commodity is the sum of imports, current production, and any carryover. Consumption is determined by summing domestic use and exports. The fundamental analyst strives to determine and evaluate the factors that are likely to exert the greatest influence on the price of the commodity.

Factors other than local demand and supply also influence the price of a commodity, and must be considered by the fundamental analyst. One of these influences is the *general commodity price level.* When the general commodity price level is unusually high or unusually low, price levels in the other markets are affected. Shifts in the value of the U.S. currency vs. foreign currencies also exert an influence on commodity prices by changing the amount of the commodity that foreign buyers can get for their money. Other external market factors include production and price controls set by the government, actions taken by international trade organizations, U.S. monetary and fiscal policy, and the general condition of the economy.

Also, the fundamental analyst has to be aware of seasonal price tendencies. For example, Chicago December wheat reaches a summer low usually in July or August, and from this low, a seasonal price advance usually occurs into at least November or December. The fundamental analyst has to be familiar with these seasonal tendencies and understand the causes responsible for these patterns.

Basic information on most active futures markets and commodities is readily available. The largest single source of information of this type is the federal government. The U.S. Department of Agriculture publishes more than a hundred reports each year on farmers' growing intentions, projected yields, forecasted demand, and actual production of agricultural commodities. Other government agencies report on nonagricultural commodities, and on such important market influences as projected and actual imports, exports, weather, and legislative action. The Federal Reserve System publishes a number of publications covering topics related to interest rates. In addition, there are many private crop and private forecasting services.

Details on reports published by the government can be obtained by writing the following agencies:

Government Printing Office
Washington, DC 20401

U.S. Department of Agriculture (GPA 507A)
14th and Independence Ave., S.W.
Washington, DC 20250

U.S. Department of the Interior
Bureau of Mines
2401 E Street, N.W.
Washington, DC 20241

Federal Reserve Board
Publications
20th and Constitution Ave., N.W.
Washington, DC 20551

The Department of Agriculture publishes a useful pamphlet that you can request: *How to Get Information from the U.S. Department of Agriculture.* Contact the Office of Information (telephone: 202-447-7451) for a copy of this pamphlet.

The futures exchanges are major sources of information on the commodities they trade. All the exchanges issue regular statistical data on prices, warehouse stocks, and market activity. In addition, many exchanges publish booklets explaining the nature and operations of their futures markets.

There are many periodicals, newsletters, and charting services that engage in forecasting futures prices. Descriptions of these periodicals are presented in *Investment Publications,* available from:

International Publishing Company, Inc.
625 Michigan Avenue
Suite 1920
Chicago, IL 60611

37

ROLE OF THE FEDERAL RESERVE BOARD

The Federal Reserve Board is our central bank, the bank that oversees the activities of the over 5,000 commercial banks that are members of the Federal Reserve System. These member banks account for 70 percent of all commercial bank deposits. With its broad supervisory authority over these banks, the Fed controls the nation's money supply. Although the Fed does not control interest rates, it can significantly influence interest rates through its control of the money supply.

The Fed uses the following tools to manage the money supply:

1. *Open-market operations.* These operations, the most flexible policy instrument the Fed has, consist of the purchase and sale of government securities (bills, notes, and bonds) on the open market. For example, when the Fed sells securities, it takes money out of the banking system. This action reduces the money supply, which puts upward pressure on interest rates. However, when the Fed buys securities, it injects money into the banking system. This loosening of the money supply reduces pressure on interest rates. These transactions are employed continuously each day as needed.

2. *Discount window.* Discounting occurs when the Fed lends reserves to member banks. The rate of interest the Fed charges is called the discount rate. The discount rate is altered periodically as market conditions change or to complement open market

operations. It is primarily of interest as an indication of the Fed's view of the economy and of credit demand.

3. *Reserve requirements.* Banks are required to maintain reserves against the money they loan. When the Fed increases reserve requirements, the amount of deposits supported by the supply of reserves is reduced and banks have to reduce the number of loans they make. This tool is the least flexible instrument the Fed has, and consequently it is seldom used.

Since reserves are not interest-bearing deposits, it is in the interest of each bank to keep only the required minimum on deposit. Once the minimum reserve requirements are met, member banks can loan excess reserve funds, known as fed funds, to banks in need of additional cash. The fed funds rate is closely watched by the financial community, because it is a short-term interest rate and generally acts as a benchmark for other short-term rates. Thus, changes in the fed funds rate have a definite influence on the prices of financial futures.

38

SPREADS

Most speculative futures transactions involve either buying futures in the expectation of benefiting from rising prices or selling futures in the expectation of benefiting from declining prices. However, numerous other strategies are available to futures participants. One relatively simple example is the use of spread positions.

A simple spread involves buying one futures contract and selling another futures contract in the same or economically related commodities. Prices of the two futures contracts have a tendency to go up and down together, and gains on one side of a spread are offset by losses on the other. The purpose of a spread is to profit from an expected change in the relationship between the purchase price of one and the selling price of the other. The Kansas City Board of Trade (KCBT), in a booklet titled *Wheat Futures,* provides an illustration of a spread.

EXAMPLE:

Suppose that a speculator expects corn prices to gain relative to hard red winter wheat prices because a severe summer drought is expected to reduce corn production. Currently, KCBT hard red winter wheat December futures are trading at a $.90 premium to December corn futures. If the speculator's expectations are borne out, the spread between corn and wheat prices will narrow. Therefore, on June 15, one December corn contract (5,000 bushels) is purchased at $3.00 and one December wheat contract (5,000 bushels) is sold at $3.90 for a spread of $.90.

Suppose that by July 15, the December corn futures price has risen to $3.25 and the December wheat futures price has risen to $4.00. The spread has narrowed to $.75, producing a profit of $.15.

	Wheat Transaction	Corn Transaction		Spread
June 15:				
Sell Dec	$3.90	—	=	$0.90
Buy Dec	—	$3.00		
July 15:				
Buy Dec	$4.00	—	=	$0.75
Sell Dec	—	$3.25		
Profit/loss	− $0.10	+ $0.25		+ $0.15

Profit per contract = $.15 × 5,000 bushels = $750

Note that because the spread moved in the expected direction, the profit from the corn transaction more than offset the loss from the wheat transaction. In trading spreads, individual price movement (up and down) is irrelevant. Profit or loss is determined only by the change in the relationship of the prices between the two commodities. Consequently, spreads are often considered more conservative and less risky than having an outright long or short futures position. Therefore, margins on spreads are lower than margins on outright purchases or sales of futures contracts.

39

TREASURY BOND FUTURES

Futures contracts can be bought for all three Treasury securities: bonds, notes, and bills. In addition, there is also a very active futures market in Eurodollars, which are U.S. dollars on deposit outside of the United States. The most actively traded futures contract from 1984 to 1993 was the contract traded on U.S. Treasury bonds. Treasury bonds are Treasury securities that mature in from ten to thirty years.

In 1994, the Chicago Mercantile Exchange (CME) Eurodollar futures overtook the Chicago Board of Trade (CBOT) Treasury bond futures as the world's most traded contract. These futures are designed to be used as a hedging vehicle for swaps. Swaps are agreements by two parties to exchange a series of cash flows in the future. This market is dominated by institutions and holds little interest for individual investors. For that reason, this key will focus upon treasury bond futures, which have more relevance to individual investors.

The popularity of these bonds can be attributed to several factors. First, the massive deficits of the U.S. government have required the issuance of many Treasury bonds. In addition, Treasury bonds have become the benchmark for long-term interest rates to which other long-term rates are tied. Thus, prices of Treasury bond futures are a sensitive barometer of long-term interest rates. Treasury bond futures are widely used to hedge against the risk of bond holding.

About 400,000 Treasury bond futures contracts were traded daily at the CBOT in 1994, up over 25 percent from the previous year. A contract is for future delivery of a $100,000 face value Treasury bond. In actuality, futures traders rarely take delivery of Treasury bonds, and most trades are canceled by making an offsetting trade.

The Treasury bond futures contract accepts delivery of U.S. Treasury securities with maturities or earliest call dates at least fifteen years in the future. Delivery is allowed at any time during the delivery month. The last day of trading is the eighth-to-the-last business day of the delivery month. The U.S. Treasury bond contract terms can be summarized as follows:

Exchange:	Chicago Board of Trade
Quantity:	$100,000 face value
Delivery months:	March, June, September, December
Delivery specifications:	Delivery of U.S. Treasury bonds with maturity value of at least 15 years if not callable, and if callable, with a first call date no earlier than 15 years from the first day of the delivery month. Call date means the first date on which the bond can be retired at the election of the issuer.
Minimum price movement:	32nds of a point, or $31.25 per contract

Many institutions have large bond holdings, which they use to hedge against interest-rate risk. A rise in interest rates pushes down the price of bonds, while declining interest rates raise bond prices. An investor who is concerned that interest rates are about to spurt upward can sell Treasury bond futures. If bond prices later decline, the price of bond futures also drops, enabling the investor to buy back the futures for less. If bond prices rise, the investor loses money on the futures but makes money on the bonds.

Inexperienced individual investors should avoid this market. Trading is dominated by institutions and dealers in Treasury securities who use sophisticated trading systems. Because this market is generally played by professionals, the margin required is usually less than that for stock index futures. Lower margin means higher leverage and greater risk.

40

PROGRAM TRADING

Program trading is a market strategy used by institutions to buy or sell vast amounts of securities. Typically, computers are programmed to evaluate the difference between the prices of actual stocks and the prices of futures contracts on an index made up of those stocks.

If the futures rise to a premium over the aggregate value of the stocks on the index, the trader can sell the futures short and buy the underlying securities, exploiting the price differential between the two. The process is reversed when the futures sell at a discount to the stocks making up the index.

For example, if the price of the S&P 500 futures contract skids substantially below the market price of the stocks that make up the index, computers trigger automatic signals to sell stocks and buy the futures. If the prices of the S&P 500 stocks lag behind the futures on the index, the computers will signal to buy these stocks and sell the futures to exploit the spread.

As a rule, the futures sell at a premium to the casn index. This is especially true in bull markets, but over the years, on average, stock prices have risen. Thus, the expectations of speculators in futures are for generally rising markets. Near expiration date, the futures and the cash index are almost equal in value.

Analysts have a formula to determine—or to take an educated guess at—the fair value of the futures. Program traders use this figure, rather than the actual cash value of the stocks, to determine when to sell and when to buy. For example, sell programs may be activated when the futures fall a point below their fair value but they are still a point above the cash value of the underlying stocks.

Different forms of program trading exist. Some involve stock indexes and the futures. Others, such as portfolio insurance, are designed to limit losses in declining markets.

Portfolio insurance is not insurance in the traditional sense. It involves a strategy to use stock index futures to protect the value of a portfolio. For example, when the market value declines, in theory, traders can offset most losses through short sales (selling futures) in the futures market. In practice, as will be explained shortly, this strategy does not always work.

Program trading has been widely criticized for contributing to market volatility. When computers signal the purchase of stocks, rounds of automatic stock orders flash onto the screens of traders, propelling the market upward. Conversely, when computers flash sell signals, stocks are dumped, and the market drops. Such trading, which has been responsible on some days for more than a quarter of total stock trading volume, is cited by critics as a factor in the October 19, 1987 crash, when the market dropped a record 23 percent.

That collapse shattered some assumptions about program trading. First, with so many investors selling stock, futures prices dropped dramatically. The plunge in futures frightened stock owners into selling, which precipitated further declines in both the futures and the stock markets.

Futures and stock prices were soon out of sync, and the gap proceeded to widen. However, both markets lost value so quickly that many orders failed to get executed at all, much less simultaneously, so that traders could not exploit the gap. By late afternoon, most program traders had ceased trading, further reducing the demand for stocks. Whether program trading contributed to the crash is still debated on Wall Street.

Whatever its impact, program trading was suspended from the NYSE for three weeks, from October 20 until November 9, 1987.

After the crash, most Wall Street firms pulled back from program trading in response to heated criticism. However, in 1988, many firms slowly resumed program trading, confident that the outcry had passed and eager to make the profits that this relatively low-risk strategy can yield. Although it doesn't inspire the headlines devoted to derivatives currently, program trading remains a major force in the stock market. In 1994, 11.5 percent of the common shares traded on the NYSE resulted from program trading.

Portfolio insurance, on the other hand, was thoroughly discredited for its failure to perform as expected during the crash. As a consequence, that insurance is no longer regarded as an important factor in the stock market.

41

DERIVATIVES

In 1994–95, the business press reported, on almost a daily basis, the risks posed by derivatives to the financial system. Awareness of these risks has been heightened by the large losses sustained by hedge funds, dealers, and some corporations that use derivatives to speculate on interest rates and currencies.

The spectacular collapse of the venerable British investment bank Barings P.L.C., in February 1995, startled the investment world. A 28-year-old futures trader in Singapore caused over $1 billion in losses by betting wrong on the Japanese stock and bond markets forcing Barings into bankruptcy.

After Gibson Greetings Inc. lost $25 million on derivative trades in 1994, it filed suit against the Bankers Trust Company, the prominent New York bank and major derivatives dealer. Procter & Gamble incurred a $157 million pretax charge against earnings from losses on derivative transactions.

The governmental sector was not immune from the list of financial casualties. Derivatives were partly blamed for a $2 billion investment fund loss for California's affluent Orange County, which filed the biggest municipal bankruptcy in history in 1994.

The mutual fund industry has also been battered by derivative losses. In an effort to increase yields, many money market mutual funds invested heavily in derivatives, often without adequate consideration of the risks involved. Money market mutual funds normally maintain a constant share price of $1, with all earnings paid in additional shares, so the value of a share never rises above $1. In June 1994, derivative losses in Bank America's Pacific Horizon money funds were so great that Bank America injected $68 million to prevent the price dropping below $1. Several other fund companies including CS First Boston and the Zweig funds have also added cash into their money funds to compensate for derivative losses.

In probably the largest bailout in the history of the mutual fund industry, PaineWebber Group disclosed in July 1994 that it would spend $180 million to rescue the PaineWebber Short-term U.S. Government Securities Fund. This followed the $88 million already spent by the brokerage firm to reimburse investors who thought they were purchasing shares in a safe and secure fund. In an effort to generate slightly higher returns, the fund invested in derivatives and was left holding unsaleable securities when interest rates rose.

The derivatives market is huge and incredibly complex. The estimated volume of worldwide derivatives outstanding as of 1995 was at least $24 trillion in terms of the notional, or principal, amount of derivative contracts.

Don't fret if you are confused by the different types of derivatives. There are now more than 1,200 different kinds of derivatives, most of which require a computer to properly evaluate. In fact, pricing and trading derivatives would be impossible without sophisticated computer systems.

Although derivative terminology can be daunting (see Exhibit 5 for an explanation of some basic terms), a broad definition is easy to grasp. Derivatives are financial instruments whose value is derived from fluctuations in the share of an underlying asset such as a share price, a rate of interest, or a currency exchange rate. Derivatives can be based upon currencies, commodities, government or corporate debt, home mortgages, stocks, interest rates, or any combination of these. Options and futures are major classes of derivatives.

Although derivatives can be used for speculative purposes, the most common use is for hedging. For example, companies often use forwards (see Exhibit 5) and exchange listed futures to protect against fluctuations in currency or commodity prices.

Forwards represent the largest component of the derivatives market due to the need by businesses to reduce the uncertainty of variable costs such as foreign-currency transactions. For example, a U.S. importer might promise to buy machinery at a future date for a price quoted in German currency. This importer can use a forward contract—or a futures contract, if one is available that meets the firm's needs—to fix the dollar cost of converting the German currency at that future date. Thus, the importer avoids a loss if the dollar cost of German currency increases between the purchase and delivery dates.

Derivatives are one of the cheapest and most effective tools a company has to protect itself against shocks in currency values, commodity prices, and interest rates. Over two thirds of the 500 largest American companies use derivatives regularly according to a recent study. Companies use them as a kind of financial insurance policy, locking in currency or interest rate values for months or years, allowing companies to plan their spending and operating budgets with some assurance.

Improperly used, however, derivatives can increase rather than reduce risk exposure. Derivative losses incurred by business firms, both from the United States and overseas, mutual funds, and even governments have heightened concerns over these financial instruments. In 1994, about $10 billion of derivative losses were reported, twice the amount disclosed in the previous ten years for such investments.

EXHIBIT 5
Trader's Language

Call:
An option that gives the buyer the right to purchase a specified quantity of an asset at a fixed price at any time during the life of the option.

Cap:
A contract that protects the holder from a rise in interest rates beyond a certain point.

Floor:
A contract that protects the holder against a decline in prices below a certain point.

Forward:
A contract obligating one party to buy, and the other party to sell, a specific asset for a fixed price at a future date.

Future:
A forward contract traded on an exchange.

Notional value:
The full value of the obligations owed by all parties involved in a derivatives contract.

Put:
An option that gives the buyer the right to sell a specified quantity of the underlying interest at a fixed price at any time during the life of the option.

Swap:
An agreement by two parties to exchange a series of cash flows in the future.

Swaption:
An option giving the holder the right to enter into or cancel a swap at a future date.

Underlying:
The asset, index, or benchmark whose price movement determines the value of the derivative.

42

OPENING A
FUTURES ACCOUNT

Futures and options on futures contracts are bought
and sold through brokerage firms. Therefore, the first
step in trading futures is selecting a broker. This decision
will be affected by your experience in and knowledge of
futures markets, and the commitment in time and effort
you plan to make in trading futures. Many futures traders
prefer to do their own research and analysis and make
their own decisions. In other words, they trade futures in
a way that is similar to the management of their own
stock portfolios. Other traders rely on the recommendations of a brokerage firm. Some traders purchase independent trading advice, and make their decisions
accordingly. Still others choose to participate in a commodity trading pool.

There is no magic formula for deciding how to participate in futures trading. Your decision should be based
on such factors as your knowledge and experience in
trading futures, the time and attention you will devote to
trading, the amount of capital you can afford to commit,
and your individual temperament and tolerance for risk.
Some individuals thrive on the fast pace of futures trading; others are unable to make the immediate decisions
that are frequently required. Some individuals accept the
fact that futures trading usually results in losses; others
lack the discipline to acknowledge a bad decision and liquidate a position.

Opening an account with a brokerage firm is not significantly different from opening a bank account. A
prospective investor has to provide his/her name,
address, occupation, social security number, citizenship,
an acknowledgment that the customer is of legal age, and

a suitable bank or financial reference. For futures traders, other information, such as financial data, is used to determine whether the individual is financially qualified to trade futures. In addition, every new account must sign a risk-disclosure statement that describes the risks associated with futures trading. If your broker does not strongly advise you of these risks, you should perhaps look for another broker.

Prospective customers are also required to sign a security-deposit statement. This agreement requires that a customer make good any losses incurred in trading. Funds deposited for margin requirements are required to be accounted for separately by a brokerage firm. By law, these segregated funds are not subject to liens against the brokerage firm. Once the funds are deposited, you may begin to trade.

The amount of money needed to start futures trading varies with the type and quantity of contracts purchased. Funds must be adequate to pay the initial margin requirement and to meet possible margin calls to replenish your account. Your broker will tell you how much money will be required initially. Some brokerage firms may ask for a customer deposit of $5,000 while others may require $25,000 or more.

43

TIPS ON TRADING FUTURES

Given the danger of trading futures, there are certain rules futures speculators should observe. The most important single characteristic of successful futures traders is that they are disciplined. They have a plan or system and they follow it. If you don't have a plan or system, you should not be trading futures. This market is not for casual investors. It is dominated by professionals who work full-time at searching for and exploiting opportunities.

Rules to follow in trading futures include the following:

1. *Select an experienced broker.* Trade only with a reputable firm that has at least one broker with extensive experience in trading futures. To select a broker, ask for the opinion of the office manager, and then arrange for an interview. Determine that he/she has appropriate experience (at least three years) and qualifications to be of assistance to you. If you are not comfortable with your broker, look elsewhere.

2. *Set your maximum risk.* Decide how much loss you are willing to accept in advance. This loss can be expressed as a specific amount or a percentage of margin. Remember that you are likely to have more losses than gains. The key to success is to cut your losses short and let your profit run.

3. *A way to force discipline is to use stop orders.* A stop order is an order that becomes a market order when a particular price level is reached. A sell stop is placed below the market; a buy stop is placed above the market.

4. *Never meet a margin call.* When your initial margin is reduced by losses, your broker will call you to deposit more margin. Do not deposit more money. Liquidate your position and accept the loss.
5. *Make dry runs for at least three months before you risk your money.* This experience is vital to making you a successful trader. Many investors plunge into this market without adequate preparation.
6. *Specialize in the futures markets.* Confine yourself to several commodities or stock index futures. The more narrow your interest, the easier it is for you to become knowledgeable.
7. *Trade in futures only what you can afford to lose.* If the loss of this money would cause loss of sleep, you don't belong in the futures market.
8. *Avoid overtrading.* If you don't see opportunities, don't trade. At certain times, futures should be avoided. Trade only when the risk-to-reward ratio is acceptable.
9. *Risk no more than 10 percent of your trading funds in any single position.* This limit will prevent the decimation of your trading capital as a result of a bad trade.
10. *Never average down.* Don't buy more contracts when you have a loss in existing contracts.

44

INFORMATION ON FUTURES

Studies have shown that most speculators in futures lose money. Hence, this market is very risky. Investors who are not willing to spend a great deal of time studying this market should avoid it altogether. Trading in futures is primarily undertaken by individuals and professionals who may spend hours each day acquiring the expertise to make successful trades.

The first place to look for information on futures are the exchanges where futures are traded. All of these exchanges have brochures explaining how the exchange works, describing the futures markets in general and the contracts they trade in particular. Some brochures even offer suggestions on trading strategies. The addresses and phone numbers of the major futures exchanges are as follows:

Chicago Board of Trade
141 West Jackson Blvd.
Chicago, IL 60604
312-435-3500

Chicago Mercantile Exchange
30 South Wacker Drive
Chicago, IL 60606
312-930-1000

Kansas City Board of Trade
4800 Main Street, Suite 303
Kansas City, MO 64112
816-753-7500

Mid-American Commodity Exchange
141 Jackson Blvd.
Chicago, IL 60604
312-341-3000

New York Futures Exchange
20 Broad Street
New York, NY 10005
212-656-4949 or 800-843-6933

New York Mercantile Exchange
4 World Trade Center, 8th Floor
New York, NY 10048
212-938-2222

Several periodicals are excellent sources of information on futures. The financial weekly *Barron's* has a column entitled "Commodities Corner," written by Cheryl S. Einhorn. This column is an excellent source of information on what is happening currently in the futures market. *Barron's* is probably the single most valuable source of statistical information on all the investment markets. A one-year subscription, which costs $135, can be obtained by writing to this address:

Barron's
200 Burnett Road
Chicopee, MA 01020

An excellent monthly magazine is *Futures,* which specializes in both commodities and options. Its discussions of different trading techniques are particularly useful. A one-year subscription, which costs $39, can be obtained by writing to the following address:

Futures
219 Parkade
Cedar Falls, IA 50613

Most speculators in futures use technical analysis to determine the best time to make trades in futures. Technical analysis assumes that prices exhibit repetitive patterns and that the recognition of these patterns can be used to identify trading opportunities. With information on variables such as price, trading volume, and open interest, the technical analyst attempts to form an opinion about the future direction of prices. Technical analysts spend a great deal of time scrutinizing price charts and searching for patterns.

A useful monthly magazine for those interested in technical analysis is *Technical Analysis of Stocks and Commodities.* This monthly magazine, which costs $64.95 for a one-year subscription, can be obtained by contacting:

Technical Analysis Inc.
3517 SW Alaska St.
Seattle, WA 98126-2791

The subject of futures can only be skimmed in a book of this size. Many excellent books are available that offer more comprehensive treatment of futures and futures trading. Beginning investors might consider *Getting Started in Futures* by Todd Lofton (John Wiley & Sons, New York, 1993). Another good book for the beginning investor is Jake Bernstein's *Facts on Futures* (Probus Publishing, Chicago, 1992). For more experienced investors, a comprehensive treatment is *The Futures Markets* by Daniel Siegel and Diane Siegel (Probus Publishing, Chicago, 1990).

QUESTIONS AND ANSWERS

Why have stock index futures become so popular with institutional and individual investors?

Trading in stock index futures began in 1982 when the Kansas City Board of Trade introduced a futures contract on the Value Line Composite Index. Today, the two main stock index futures contracts traded in the United States are the Standard & Poor's 500 contract at the Chicago Mercantile Exchange (CME) (by far the most popular index futures contract) and the New York Stock Exchange Index contract at the New York Futures Exchange (NYFE).

Investors have found stock index futures contracts to be an efficient vehicle for trading on expectations of future general movements in the equity market. Stock index futures permit investors to participate in broad market movements without having to individually acquire hundreds of different stocks. Index futures also enable investors to hedge their portfolios against short-term losses by selling futures short. This strategy is often preferable to disrupting the portfolio by temporarily selling off individual stocks.

What are some of the basic positions you can assume when trading futures?

The principal strategies you can employ in trading futures are to "go long," to "go short," and "to spread." Going long means buying a futures contract in anticipation of a price increase. The opposite of going long is going short, which means selling a futures contract in anticipation of a price decrease. A spread position is the simultaneous purchase and sale of futures contracts in different months, or in different markets, hoping that a price differential between the two will result in a profit.

Positions in the futures market are closed out by taking the opposite action of the initial position. Thus, a long position is closed out by a sale of the same contract month, a short position is liquidated by a purchase of the same contract month, and a spread position is eliminated by simultaneously buying and selling in the opposite way to the initial action.

What is the significance of daily price limits for futures?

Each exchange sets limits within which a future's price can fluctuate during a single trading session. This restriction serves to limit the exposure of traders on any single trading day. The exchange determines the price ranges based upon variations occurring in the underlying cash markets. These ranges can be adjusted periodically as price volatility increases or decreases. In some contracts, daily price limits are eliminated during the month in which the contract expires. Prices are particularly volatile during the expiration month. As a result, inexperienced traders may wish to liquidate prior to that time.

The limits are expressed in terms of the previous day's closing price plus and minus an amount per trading unit. When a futures price has risen by its daily limit, there can be no trading at any higher price until the next day of trading. Alternatively, when a futures price has declined by its daily limit, there can be no trading at any lower price until the next day of trading. Therefore, if the daily limit for a particular grain is currently $.10 a bushel and the previous day's settlement price was $3.50, no trading can occur during the current day at any price below $3.40 or above $3.60. The price is allowed to increase or decrease only by the limit amount each day.

How can options be used to hedge against a decline in the market price of common stock?

Two common strategies are covered call writing and buying puts. Covered call writing involves writing calls against common stock you already own. Premiums earned from writing call options provide both cash flow and price protection. The protection from a decline in the price of the common stock is limited to the amount of the premium.

EXAMPLE:
An investor paid $60 a share for 100 shares of XYZ common stock. He receives $4 a share by writing a call against that stock. If the price drops to $58 a share, the $2 decline is more than offset by the $4 premium. The investor is ahead by $2 a share and is protected down to $56. A net loss is incurred if the stock falls below $56 at expiration.

The other common hedging strategy involves the purchase of put options. Speculative stocks typically involve greater risk in the pursuit of large profits. Buying put options reduces the risk of acquiring such stocks while still maintaining the upside potential of the stock.

EXAMPLE:
The common stock of XYZ currently sells at $60. XYZ is a very speculative stock, but an investor expects a sharp run-up in its price in the next several months. To reduce the risk that the stock may instead drop sharply, he/she pays $3 a share to purchase a put with the exercise price of $60. The put limits the potential loss to $3 a share. If the stock price rises sharply, the investor's profit is reduced by the $3 share cost of the put. The reduction in profit is even less if the investor is able to sell the put while it has some remaining time value.

What are the major variables influencing options premiums?

An at-the-money option (price of the common stock equals the exercise price) usually has the greatest time value. An out-of-the-money option usually has less time value because there is less likelihood of profitably exercising the option. Because of the reduced opportunity for leverage, a substantially in-the-money option usually also has less time value. Its premium is predominantly a reflection of its intrinsic value.

An option is a "wasting asset," since it is has no value after expiration. An option's time value and premium are influenced by the length of time remaining until expiration. Therefore, the longer the time remaining, the greater the time value.

The volatility of the underlying common stock also affects the option premium. The more volatile the price of the underlying common stock, the greater the option premium. If other factors remain unchanged, a substantial increase in the volatility of the underlying common stock will expand an option's premium.

Ultimately, option premiums are determined by supply and demand. The supply results from the willingness of traders and investors to write (or sell) options, and the demand stems from the interest of other traders and investors in buying options. Not surprisingly, the demand for call options normally climbs when stock prices are rising and the demand for put options normally jumps when stock prices are slipping.

What are the similarities and dissimilarities of options as compared to stocks?

Options share certain similarities with common stocks. Among these are the following:

1. Both options and stock investors can follow price movements, trading volume, and other significant information day by day or even minute by minute. The buyer or seller of an option, like the buyer or seller of common stock, can learn almost

instantly the price at which an order has been executed.

2. Both options and common stocks are listed securities. Orders to buy and sell options are transacted through brokers in the same way as orders to buy and sell common stock. In addition, orders are executed on the trading floor of a national, SEC-regulated exchange in an open, competitive auction market.

Some important differences exist between options and common stocks:

1. Options differ from common stocks in that they are "wasting assets." Common stock can be held indefinitely in the hope that its value may eventually increase. If an option is not closed out or exercised prior to its expiration date, it is worthless and the holder loses the entire premium.

2. Unlike common stock, there are no certificates evidencing ownership. Instead, positions in options are indicated on printed statements prepared by brokerage firms.

3. Unlike shares of common stock, there is no fixed number of options available. The number of outstanding options is determined by the number of buyers and sellers interested in receiving and selling these rights.

4. Common stock ownership provides the owner with an ownership interest in the company, voting rights, and rights to any dividends distributed. However, an option owner's potential benefit is defined solely by possible movement in the price of a stock.

What does margin mean in the context of futures?

Every futures trader should understand two margin-related terms: initial margin and maintenance margin. Initial margin is the cash that must be deposited with the broker for each futures contract as a guarantee of the fulfillment of the contract. If profits accrue on an open futures position, the profits are added to the balance in a margin account. If losses accrue on a given day, the losses are deducted from the balance in a margin account.

If the balance in a margin account is reduced below a certain level (known as the "maintenance margin"), a broker will require the deposit of additional funds to bring the account back to its initial margin. Requests for additional margin are known as margin calls.

EXAMPLE:

Suppose that the initial margin to buy a futures contract is $4,000 and that the maintenance margin is $3,000. Should losses on an open position reduce the balance in an account to $2,400, a margin call will be made for $1,600 needed to restore the account to $4,000.

Each exchange sets its own rules for maintenance margin. Generally, additional margin is required when an unfavorable price movement has reduced the initial margin in the position down to 60 to 75 percent of its original value. Maintenance margin calls must be met promptly. If a margin call is not met, the customer's position can be liquidated to meet the margin call

What are the different types of spreads in futures trading?

A spread is the simultaneous purchase and sale of futures contracts for the same commodity or instrument for delivery in different months, or in different but related markets. The simplest spread is the simultaneous purchase of a long position in one futures contract and a short position in a different but related futures contract. Spreads are established to profit from a change in the difference between the prices of the two contracts. Because gains and losses occur only as the result of a change in the price difference rather than changes in the absolute prices of the futures contracts, spreads are usually more conservative and less risky than having an outright long or short futures position.

There are three basic types of spreads:

1. The intramarket spread. This is the most common type of spread and consists of a long position in one contract month and a short position in a different contract month of the same commodity on the same exchange. An example of an intramarket spread would be long December corn/short March corn on the Chicago Board of Trade.
2. The intermarket spread. This spread involves buying futures contracts on one exchange and selling the same contract on another exchange. An example would be long wheat on the Chicago Board of Trade and short wheat on the Kansas City Board of Trade.
3. The intercommodity spread. This spread involves a long position in one commodity and a short position in a related commodity. An example would be long oats/short corn.

What is the role of the Options Clearing Corporation?

Standardized options are issued by the Options Clearing Corporation (OCC), a clearing agency regulated by the Securities and Exchange Commission. The OCC guarantees that the terms of an options contract will be fulfilled. An options buyer looks to the OCC rather than to any particular options writer for performance. In a similar vein, the obligations of options writers are owed to the OCC rather than to any particular buyer.

When there are matching orders from a buyer and seller, the OCC severs the link between the parties. In effect, the OCC guarantees contract performance by becoming the buyer to the seller and the seller to the buyer. As a result, the seller can buy back the same option he/she has written, and this action has no effect on the rights of the original buyer to sell, hold, or exercise his/her option.

GLOSSARY

American-style option an option that can be exercised by the holder at any time after it is purchased until it expires.

At-the-money option an option whose exercise price is equal to the price of the underlying common stock.

Basis the difference between the futures price and the current cash price of a commodity or security.

Bear one who believes prices are headed lower.

Bear spread an investing position in which the option with a lower exercise price is sold, and the option with a higher exercise price is bought.

Bull one who believes prices are headed higher.

Bull spread an investing position that involves the purchase of an option with a lower exercise price, and the sale of an option with a higher exercise price.

Call option an option that gives the buyer the right to purchase a specified quantity of the underlying interest at a fixed price at any time during the life of the option.

Cap a contract that protects the holder from a rise in interest rates beyond a certain point.

CBOE (Chicago Board Options Exchange) the world's largest options exchange.

CBOT (Chicago Board of Trade) the largest futures exchange

CME (Chicago Mercantile Exchange) the second largest futures exchange.

Commodity futures a contract covering the purchase and sale of physical commodities for future delivery on a commodity exchange.

Contract month the month a contract matures; the delivery month.

Cover the closing out of a short position.

Covered call writing the writing of a call by someone who owns the shares of stock on which he/she has written the call.

Delta a measure of the change in an option's price compared to the change in the underlying price of the stock.

Derivative instruments financial instruments whose value is derived from the stocks, bonds, indexes, currencies, etc., upon which they are based.

European-style option an option that may be exercised only on the expiration date.

Exercise price the price at which the holder can sell to or buy from the writer the item underlying an option.

Financial futures a futures contract that involves the delivery of financial securities or cash to fulfill the contract.

Firm-specific risk risk that results from factors peculiar to an individual company.

Floor a contract that protects the holder against a decline in prices below a certain point.

Floor broker an exchange member who executes trades for the accounts of others.

Fundamental analysis prediction of future prices based upon an analysis of demand and supply.

Future an agreement between two parties that commits one party to sell a commodity or security to the other at a given price and on a specified future date.

Hedging the purchase and sale of options and futures solely for the purpose of establishing a known price level.

Industry risk the risk that results from developments unique to an industry.

In-the-money options a call is in the money when the exercise price is less than the market price; a put is in the money when the exercise price is greater than the market price.

Intrinsic value the amount of money, if any, that could be realized by exercising the option.

LEAPS options on individual stocks and indexes that provide the owner the right to purchase or sell shares of a stock at a specified price on or before a given date up to three years in the future.

Limit the maximum amount a futures price may move, up or down, in any one trading session.

Limit order a trade that can be executed only at a specific price.

Liquidation the closing out of a long position.

Long the purchase of a futures contract to establish a market position that has not been closed out through an offsetting sale; the opposite of short.

Maintenance margin the amount of money that must be maintained on deposit while a futures position is open.

Margin in futures trading, a good-faith deposit to guarantee fulfillment of the purchase or sale obligation.

Margin call a demand for additional cash because of an unfavorable movement in price.

Market order an order stipulating that a move should be executed at the best price currently available.

Market risk the risk that results from overall movements of the market.

Moving average an average that is updated by dropping the first number and adding in the last number.

Naked option same as uncovered option.

Open interest the number of contracts outstanding or unliquidated at the end of a day.

Option a contract that provides to its holder (buyer) the right to purchase from or sell to the issuer (writer) a specified interest at a designated price, called the exercise price (striking price), for a given period of time.

Options buyer or holder the investor who obtains the right specified in an options contract.

Options on futures options that give the buyer the right, but not the obligation, to buy or sell a particular futures contract at a stated price at any time prior to a specified date.

Options writer the seller or issuer of an options contract.

Out-of-the-money option a call is out of the money when the exercise price is greater than the market price; a put is out of the money when the exercise price is lower than the market price.

Point the minimum price fluctuation of a contract.

Position an interest in the market in the form of open contracts, either long or short.

Premium the price paid by the buyer of an option to the seller of an option.

Program trading a mechanical trading system in which computers are programmed to buy or sell vast amounts of securities.

Protective puts the simultaneous purchase of a stock and a put option or the purchase of a put related to a stock already owned by the investor.

Put option an option that gives the buyer the right to sell a specified quantity of the underlying interest at a fixed price at any time during the life of the option.

Short a futures contract sold to establish a market position that has not been closed out through an offsetting purchase; the opposite of long.

Speculating assuming the price risk that hedgers are seeking to minimize.

Spreads the purchase and sale of options on the same underlying stock but with a different expiration date and/or a different exercise price.

Stop order an order to buy or sell at the market when a specific price is reached, either above or below the price that prevailed when the order was given.

Straddle the simultaneous purchase of a put and a call on the same stock with the identical expiration price and expiration month.

Striking price same as exercise price.

Swap an agreement by two parties to exchange a series of cash flows in the future.

Technical analysis attempts to predict future price movements by analyzing the past sequence of prices, volume, etc.

Tick same as point.

Time value the amount of money buyers are willing to pay for an option in the expectation that sometime before it expires it will become profitable to exercise or sell.

Uncovered call writing an options trading strategy in which the investor does not own the shares of the common stock represented by the option.

Uncovered option option contract where the owner does not hold the underlying investment.

Uncovered put writing an options strategy wherein the investor does not have a corresponding short stock position or has deposited cash or cash equivalents equal to the exercise value of the put.

Writer someone who sells an option.

APPENDIX 1

January Sequential Cycle

Jan	Feb	Mar	Apr	Jul
Feb	Mar	Apr	Jul	Oct
Mar	Apr	May	Jul	Oct
Apr	May	June	Jul	Oct
May	Jun	Jul	Oct	Jan
Jun	Jul	Aug	Oct	Jan
Jul	Aug	Sep	Oct	Jan
Aug	Sep	Oct	Jan	Apr
Sep	Oct	Nov	Jan	Apr
Oct	Nov	Dec	Jan	Apr
Nov	Dec	Jan	Apr	Jul
Dec	Jan	Feb	Apr	Jul

February Sequential Cycle

Jan	Feb	Mar	May	Aug
Feb	Mar	Apr	May	Aug
Mar	Apr	May	Aug	Nov
Apr	May	Jun	Aug	Nov
May	Jun	Jul	Aug	Nov
Jun	Jul	Aug	Nov	Feb
Jul	Aug	Sep	Nov	Feb
Aug	Sep	Oct	Nov	Feb
Sep	Oct	Nov	Feb	May
Oct	Nov	Dec	Feb	May
Nov	Dec	Jan	Feb	May
Dec	Jan	Feb	May	Aug

March Sequential Cycle

Jan	Feb	Mar	Jun	Sep
Feb	Mar	Apr	Jun	Sep
Mar	Apr	May	Jun	Sep
Apr	May	Jun	Sep	Dec
May	Jun	Jul	Sep	Dec
Jun	Jul	Aug	Sep	Dec
Jul	Aug	Sep	Dec	Mar
Aug	Sep	Oct	Dec	Mar
Sep	Oct	Nov	Dec	Mar
Oct	Nov	Dec	Mar	Jun
Nov	Dec	Jan	Mar	Jun
Dec	Jan	Feb	Mar	Jun

APPENDIX 2

Specifications for All Equity Options

Unit of Trade: 100 shares per option contract.

Premium Quotations: Stated in points and fractions. One point equals $100. Minimum tick for series trading below 3 is $\frac{1}{16}$ ($6.25), and for all other series, $\frac{1}{8}$ ($12.50).

Strike Price Intervals: 2½ points for stocks trading below $25, 5 points for those trading from $25 to $200, and 10 points for those trading above $200.

Exercise Style: American-style—option may be exercised on any business day prior to the expiration date.

Expiration Months: Two near-term months plus two additional months of the January, February, or March quarterly cycle.

Expiration Dates: The Saturday immediately following the third Friday of the expiration month.

Position Limits: Limits vary according to the number of outstanding shares and trading volume. The largest, most frequently traded stocks have an option position limit of 10,500 contracts; smaller capitalization stocks may offer position limits of 7500 or 4500 contracts. Customer hedge exemptions are available.

Minimum Customer Margin for Uncovered Writers: The dollar amount of the premium plus 20% of the underlying security value minus the amount by which the option is out-of-the-money (if any) with a minimum of the premium plus 10% of the underlying security value.

Trading Hours: 9:30 A.M. to 4:10 P.M. (Eastern Time).

Exercise Settlement Price: Strike price times $100.

Exercise Settlement Time: Exercise notices tendered on any business day will result in delivery of the underlying stock on the fifth business day following exercise.

Specifications for Equity LEAPS®

Exchanges: Amex, CBOE, PHLX, PSE
Description: Equity LEAPS® are American-style options on certain equities that have terms of up to three years. With the exception of the specifications listed below, Equity LEAPS® specifications are the same as those for regular-term equity options. Equity LEAPS® have unique symbols to distinguish them from their corresponding regular-term options. Options expiring in 1995 generally being with a V, those expiring in 1996 generally begin with an L and options expiring in 1997 generally begin with a Z.
Strike Prices: Initial strike prices are set at approximately 25% above, at, and 20% below the underlying stock's price.
Expiration Dates: All Equity LEAPS® expire in January.
Position and Exercise Limits: Positions must be aggregated with those of any other option on the same underlying security for the purpose of position and exercise limits.

Specifications for Long-Term Equity Options

Exchange: NYSE
Description: Long-term equity options are American-style options on certain equities that have terms of up to three years. With the exception of the specifications listed below, long-term equity options specifications are the same as those for regular-term equity options. Long-term equity options have unique symbols to distinguish them from their corresponding regular-term options. Options expiring in 1995 generally begin with a V, those expiring in 1996 generally begin with an L and options expiring in 1997 generally begin with a Z.
Strike Prices: Initial strike prices are set at approximately 25% above, at, and 20% below the underlying stock's price.

Expiration Dates: NYSE long-term equity options expire in January of the designated year.

Position and Exercise Limits: Positions must be aggregated with those of any other option on the same underlying security for the purpose of position and exercise limits.

Standard Specifications for All Index Options

Unit of Trade: One contract equals $100 (the index multiplier) times the index level.

Premium Quotations: Stated in points and fractions. One point equals $100. Minimum tick for series trading below 3 is ¹⁄₁₆ ($6.25), and for all other series, ⅛ ($12.50). NYA options have a minimum tick of ¹⁄₁₆ for all series.

Strike Price Intervals: Generally, index options are listed at 5 point intervals to bracket the current value of the index. NYA and MID options are also listed at selective 2½ points intervals in the nearest two months. Generally, Index LEAPS® are listed at 2½ point intervals. FSX, NDX and RUT options are listed in 5 point intervals. SPQ options are listed in 10 point intervals. SPX options may be listed with up to 25 point intervals in the far-term months. OEX options are listed in 10 point intervals in the far-term month. SPL options are only listed in 25 point intervals. JPN options with more than one year to expiration are listed in 50 point intervals.

Exercise Style: Index options are designated as either American-style or European-style. American-style options can be exercised on any business day prior to expiration. European-style options can be exercised only on the last trading day prior to expiration.

Expiration Dates: The Saturday immediately following the third Friday of the expiration month

Exercise Settlement Price: The dollar difference between the index number and the strike price of tne contract, multiplied by 100. The index number is generally determined following the close of trading on the day the exercise notice is submitted. The exceptions are expiring XII, CMR, CYC, XTC, XBD, XNG, MID, DRG BTK,

EUR, JPN, TCX, NYA, SFX, BKX, NDX, RUT, BGX, BIX, CEX, CWX, EVX, GAX, MCX, IUX, RLX and TRX options which settle on the opening prices of underlying stocks in the index on the day after the last day of trading (symbol CSO for CMR, CYO for CYC, XTV for XTC, EUV for EUR, JPV for JPN, XBS for XBD, NGV for XNG, XSV for XII, MIV for MID, DRO for DRG, BTS for BTK, NYX for NYA options, NNX for NNA, RLS for RUT, BGS for BGX, BBS for BIX, CXS for CEX, CWS for CWX, EVS for EVX, GXS for GAX, HCS for HCX, IUS for IUX, RRS for RLX, TRS for TRX, TXS for TCX, NDS for NDX, BKO for BKX, and SET for SPX options). JPN, FSX and EUR options have several unique exercise settlement characteristics which are described in their respective sections.

Exercise Settlement Time: Exercise notices tendered will result in the delivery of cash on the next business day.

Trading Hours: 9:30 A.M. to 4:15 P.M. (Eastern Time) for broad-based indices (HKO, CMR, CYC, FNC, JPN, MID, CPO, CPS, FSX, NDX, LRU, LSX, LSY, LSZ, OEX, OBX, OCX, OLX, RUT, SPQ, VRU, WRU, NYA, NNA, SPL, EUR, SPX, VLE, XMI, XII, XOC) or 9:30 A.M. to 4:10 P.M. (Eastern Time) for industry specific indices (BTK, BKX, UTY, XAU, XCI, XOI, DRG, BGX, BIX, CEX, CWX, EVX, GAX, HCX, IUX, RLX, XTC, TRX, LBG, VBG, XBD, XNG and WBG).

Minimum Customer Margin for Uncovered Writers: For broad-based indices: the dollar amount of the premium plus 15% of the current underlying index value (index number × $100) minus the amount by which the option is out-of-the-money (if any) with a minimum of the premium plus 10% of the current index value. For industry specific indices: the dollar amount of the premium plus 20% of the current underlying index value (index number × $100) minus the amount by which the option is out-of-the-money (if any) with a minimum of the premium plus 10% of the current index value.

INDEX

135

BARRON'S BUSINESS KEYS Each "key" explains approximately 50 concepts and provides a glossary and index. Each book: Paperback, approx. 160 pp., 4 7/16" x 7", $4.95, Can. $6.50.

Available at bookstores, or by mail from Barron's. Enclose check or money order for full amount plus sales tax where applicable and 15% for postage & handling (minimum charge $4.95). Prices subject to change without notice. $ = U.S. dollars • Can. $ = Canadian dollars • Barron's ISBN Prefix 0-8120

Barron's Educational Series, Inc.
250 Wireless Boulevard • Hauppauge, NY 11788
In Canada: Georgetown Book Warehouse
34 Armstrong Avenue, Georgetown, Ont. L7G 4R9
www.barronseduc.com

(#10) R 1/98

More selected BARRON'S titles:

BARRON'S ACCOUNTING HANDBOOK, 2nd Ed.
Joel G. Siegel and Jae K. Shim
Provides accounting rules, guidelines, formulas and techniques etc., to help
students and business professionals work out accounting problems.
Hardcover: $29.95, Canada $38.95/ISBN 0-8120-6449-6, 880 pages

REAL ESTATE HANDBOOK, 4th Ed.
Jack P. Friedman and Jack C. Harris
A dictionary/reference for everyone in real estate. Defines approximately 2000 legal,
financial, and architectural terms. Hardcover, $29.95,
Canada $38.95/ ISBN 0-8120-6592-1, approx. 780 pages

HOW TO PREPARE FOR THE REAL ESTATE LICENSING EXAMINATIONS SALESPERSON AND BROKER, 5th Ed.
Bruce Lindeman and Jack P. Friedman
Reviews current exam topics and features updated model exams and supplemental exams,
all with explained answers.
Paperback, $12.95, Canada $16.95/ISBN 0-8120-2994-1, 340 pages

BARRON'S FINANCE AND INVESTMENT HANDBOOK 4th ED.
John Downes and Jordan Elliot Goodman
This hard-working handbook of essential information defines more than 3000 key terms, and
explores 30 basic investment opportunities. The investment information is thoroughly up-to-date.
Hardcover $35.00, Canada $45.50/ISBN 0-8120-6465-8, 1392 pages

FINANCIAL TABLES FOR MONEY MANAGEMENT
Stephen S. Solomon, Dr. Clifford Marshall, Martin Pepper, Jack P. Friedman and Jack C. Harris
Pocket-sized handbooks of interest and investment rate tables used easily by average
investors and mortgage holders.
Each book: Paperback.
Real Estate Loans, 2nd Ed., $7.95, Canada $10.50/0-8120-1618-1, 336 pages
Mortgage Payments, 2nd Ed., $6.95, Canada $8.95/0-8120-1386-7, 304 pages
Bonds, 2nd Ed., $5.95, Canada $7.50/0-8120-4995-0, 256 pages
Canadian Mortgage Payments, 2nd Ed., Canada $8.95/0-8120-1617-3, 336 pages
Adjustable Rate Mortgages, 2nd Ed., $7.95, Canada $10.50/0-8120-1529-0, 288 pages

Books may be purchased at your bookstore or by mail from Barron's. Enclose check or money order for total
amount plus sales tax where applicable and 15% for postage and handling (minimum charge $4.95). Prices
subject to change without notice.

 Barron's Educational Series, Inc.
250 Wireless Blvd., Hauppauge, NY 11788
In Canada: Georgetown Book Warehouse
34 Armstrong Ave., Georgetown, Ontario L7G 4R9
www.barronseduc.com

(•11) R1/98